CU00797937

The Battles of
Antiochus the Great

The Battles of Antiochus the Great

The failure of combined arms at Magnesia that handed the world to Rome

Graham Wrightson

Pen & Sword
MILITARY

First published in Great Britain in 2022 by
Pen & Sword Military
An imprint of
Pen & Sword Books Ltd
Yorkshire – Philadelphia

Copyright © Graham Wrightson 2022

ISBN 978 1 52679 346 1

The right of Graham Wrightson to be identified as Author of this work
has been asserted by him in accordance with the Copyright, Designs
and Patents Act 1988.

A CIP catalogue record for this book is
available from the British Library.

All rights reserved. No part of this book may be reproduced or
transmitted in any form or by any means, electronic or mechanical
including photocopying, recording or by any information storage and
retrieval system, without permission from the Publisher in writing.

Typeset by Mac Style
Printed and bound in the UK by CPI Group (UK) Ltd,
Croydon, CR0 4YY.

Pen & Sword Books Limited incorporates the imprints of Atlas,
Archaeology, Aviation, Discovery, Family History, Fiction, History,
Maritime, Military, Military Classics, Politics, Select, Transport,
True Crime, Air World, Frontline Publishing, Leo Cooper, Remember
When, Seaforth Publishing, The Praetorian Press, Wharncliffe
Local History, Wharncliffe Transport, Wharncliffe True Crime
and White Owl.

For a complete list of Pen & Sword titles please contact

PEN & SWORD BOOKS LIMITED
47 Church Street, Barnsley, South Yorkshire, S70 2AS, England
E-mail: enquiries@pen-and-sword.co.uk
Website: www.pen-and-sword.co.uk

Or

PEN AND SWORD BOOKS
1950 Lawrence Rd, Havertown, PA 19083, USA
E-mail: Uspen-and-sword@casematepublishers.com
Website: www.penandswordbooks.com

Dedication

For dearest papa.
Sorry you didn't get to see this.
In pace requiescas.
5 December 1951 to 6 December 2020

Contents

List of Illustrations

Acknowledgements

I would like to thank my wife for her constant support and for allowing me to escape the COVID-19 childcare duties for a few hours a day to write this volume. I want especially to thank my students for helping me construct the sarissas and for marching around with them as their final exam and allowing me to take pictures. I want to thank Dan Powers and Jeffrey Rop for reading a few of the sections to make sure I was not barking up the wrong tree. Also I want to thank my brother-in-law Eric Howell for his suggestions on the maps and battle diagrams. Finally, I want to thank my children, Marcus and Alexa, for not disturbing their daddy's writing too often!

Introduction

This volume examines in detail the tactical ability of Antiochus III the Great in his largest defeat, the Battle of Magnesia, as well as his other major engagements. The defeat at Magnesia allowed Rome to achieve dominance of the Eastern Mediterranean and began the slow decline of the Seleucid Empire. The main thesis is that despite his leadership and large army, Antiochus lost for one main reason: his failure to properly utilize combined arms. The theory of combined arms is a modern military term recently used as a method of comparison for ancient warfare. Through this theoretical lens it is easy to see how different generals are successful or not at getting the most out of large armies made up of varied constituent parts. Such a large army was Antiochus' strength, but his inability to use it efficiently through combined arms was repeatedly his downfall. The best and consequentially most devastating example of this is the Battle of Magnesia ad Sipylum.

Antiochus III, the ruler of the Seleucid Kingdom for the four decades either side of the turn of the second century BCE, ruled a powerful state for a long time.[1] He fought and won many battles from India to Egypt, and he lost almost as many. Compared with other Hellenistic monarchs of Macedonian-founded kingdoms, Antiochus had more diverse manpower that he could field in his army. He was in a unique position among the other kings in that he had access to the traditional infantry-based Greek cultures in Asia Minor as well as the cavalry-dominant cultures of Mesopotamia and Western Asia. Yet despite these advantages, Antiochus repeatedly came up short on the battlefield and his tactical shortcomings were no more obviously laid bare than at the Battle of Magnesia ad Sipylum. There his huge combined army, one of the largest ever fielded by Hellenistic rulers, was soundly thrashed by the smaller Roman force.

Through an analysis of Antiochus' army, the inherited standard tactics of Macedonian-style armies reliant on the sarissa phalanx and a detailed examination of the main battles of Antiochus III, this book will show how it was a lack of combined arms at its fullest realization, integrated warfare, that led to defeat at Magnesia.

Part 1: The Hellenistic Sarissa Phalanx

The Sarissa

Macedon emerged as a major force in Greek politics with Philip II and his successful implementation of the sarissa phalanx and combined arms tactics (using every type of unit together in combination).[2] His greatest success at the Battle of Chaeronea in 338 BCE demonstrated the tactical superiority of these new military developments over hoplite-centred warfare.[3] The long pike or sarissa as a weapon allowed the soldiers wielding it a much greater range of attack over the hoplite. Sarissas under Philip II and his more famous son Alexander the Great were around 15ft in length.[4] A Greek hoplite's spear, or dory, was only 8ft in length.[5] Though both Greeks and Macedonians fought in a phalanx formation, the length of the sarissas allowed for the spearheads of the first five ranks to reach the front line of the enemy. A hoplite could only attack the soldier opposite him in the enemy front line. That greater reach was the principal advantage of the sarissa-armed phalangite over the hoplite.

Sarissas also provided greater penetrative power than spears. Using two hands because of the sarissa's 14lb weight, the phalangite could lean and put his whole body force into his attack rather than the one-shoulder attack of a single-handed spear. With small heads shaped like medieval armour-piercing arrows, much the same as medieval pike heads, a sarissa thrust could puncture armour and shields more easily.[6] The Romans in battle against the Macedonian phalanx of Perseus at the Battle of Pydna in 167 BCE commented on the horrific injuries caused by the sarissas, such as punctured lungs and vital organs.[7] If sarissas had wide leaf-shaped blades the length of a small dagger, as one interpretation of the archaeological evidence suggests,[8] the phalangite could utilize his sarissa to thrust past the head of an enemy and then draw the long blade backwards, thus slicing at the exposed neck under the helmet. Similarly he could aim at the exposed legs and groin under an enemy's shield. Severing either the femoral or carotid artery would cause the enemy to bleed out in a few minutes, and even minor cuts to the legs or knees would hinder the enemy's movement. In an offensive manner the sarissa was a formidable weapon.

Though the sarissa as a weapon has such great reach and penetration, its effectiveness depends entirely on maintaining distance from the enemy. If the enemy can get inside the sarissa head, he can close on the soldier without fear of defence or counterattack. The only option a soldier had in this case was to drop the sarissa and draw a short sword for close-in personal protection. This is why the sarissa was a next-to-useless weapon in individual combat. One of the Greeks in Alexander the Great's army challenged a Macedonian to a one-on-one duel. The Greek, fighting naked and armed only with a club, easily defeated the sarissa-armed soldier by avoiding the first strike, closing the distance and throwing him to the ground (Diodorus 17.100). The sarissa was only effective in battle if used in a tightly-packed formation such as the phalanx.

The Phalanx

The phalanx was a formation that featured one rank of eight to sixteen soldiers fighting side by side with eight or sixteen other ranks. In close order, as opposed to the more open marching order, soldiers in a phalanx stood within 3ft of the man in the next rank. In a hoplite phalanx this allowed the soldier to shield the man next to him with his large 3ft-diameter shield. A soldier using a sarissa could not hold a large shield as he needed both hands to hold the weapon. So instead, phalangites (soldiers in the sarissa phalanx) attached to their left shoulder a small 2ft-diameter shield. In a sarissa phalanx the tightness of the ranks was not necessary in order to gain protection from a neighbour's shield. Rather, it was to keep the ranks tight and prevent gaps from appearing in the formation.

The phalanx formation added to the power of the sarissa. With so many men close together advancing methodically in unison, the sarissa phalanx was an awe-inspiring sight. The sarissa heads of the first five ranks would appear before the front rank and the others of the ranks behind would point upwards to deflect arrows. Even a 1in or 2in movement of the raised sarissa with the hands causes the blade on the end to move 3 or 4ft from side to side, thus impeding most missiles. For the enemy witnessing the advance of the phalanx it would seem like a large shiny hedge of iron approaching with every step. Such was the sight that many soldiers ran

The Battles of Antiochus the Great

before making contact, and horses – and likely also elephants[9] refused point-blank to attack the phalanx head-on.

As long as the sarissa phalanx stayed together and advanced slowly it was an impenetrable obstacle for the enemy to overcome. However, once the tight formation of the phalanx began to break apart the enemy could attack the resultant gaps. Usually extremely rough or uneven terrain would cause the phalanx formation to break apart. This is what happened at the Battle of Pydna when the phalanx came down from the steep riverbanks that were impassable in places. The Romans, using their short swords known as gladii (s. gladius), benefited from the gaps to hack their way deep into the ranks of the sarissa phalanx. However, before the gaps began to appear the sarissa phalanx caused significant carnage in the Roman lines.[10] At the Battle of Issus Alexander the Great's whole expedition into Persia almost unravelled completely when an impassable section of the riverbank caused a large gap to appear in the sarissa phalanx. The Greek mercenaries fighting for Persia stormed into the gap and threatened to completely rout the whole phalanx. Alexander's officers plugged the gap, but only after much effort that saw the regimental commander and over a hundred notable Macedonians killed (Arrian, *Anabasis* 2.10.7).

In Hellenistic warfare there are very few instances of artillery used on a battlefield, but this too could have disrupted the phalanx formation. On the first occasion when sources confirm the use of catapults in Greek battles, Philip II of Macedon had to retreat from an assault on a mountainside because the catapult missiles did so much damage to his infantry.[11] The Romans did often utilize field artillery, but apparently not in any battles against the various Macedonian-style armies they fought and usually defeated.

As long as the subordinate units or sections of an army's phalanx remained together and moved forward at a steady pace, the enemy could find no way through the hedge of sarissas. The only option was then to attack the sides and rear of the phalanx. A phalanx as a tightly-packed and front-facing formation was always vulnerable on its flanks. It took soldiers in a hoplite phalanx, using smaller spears but larger shields, a few seconds to change facing if confronted with an attack from the rear or sides. If they were already pushing on the rank in front with their large shields and overlapping their neighbour for protection, it could take minutes. A hoplite would have to persuade the rear ranks to step back and stop pressing so tightly, pull back or lift up his shield so as not to collide with the soldiers around him and then turn in one swift movement to face the direction of the enemy attack. We know that such rapid turns were part of a soldier's drill, just as they are in all modern military exercises today. However, to execute such turns in the midst of a tight phalanx and the melee of hand-to-hand combat took incredible discipline and training. Even in the elite army of Sparta, only the few full Spartan regiments of the *Homoioi*, or 'Similars', were able to do so. As a result, most hoplite phalanxes simply fled when attacked from the flanks or rear.

For a soldier in a sarissa phalanx changing facing was even more difficult to accomplish in battle. Though they had a smaller shield that never came into contact with their neighbour in the phalanx, a sarissa phalangite had to contend with the extra length of their sarissa. It is a very fast manoeuvre to turn sideways or to the rear when holding a sarissa and a shield. You just lift up the sarissa until it is vertical and then turn. The difficulty arises in making sure that every soldier in each rank carries out the manoeuvre at the same time. If even one does not, then the long weapons can get tangled together. In turning to face the rear directly, only each rank of eight or sixteen in the phalanx has to turn together, but if turning to face an attack from the sides, the whole phalanx either has to raise their sarissas together and turn 90 degrees and then lower the sarissas together, or the whole phalanx has to march towards the oncoming attack while slowly adjusting their facing to be directly opposing the enemy. In a phalanx that usually numbered 16,000 soldiers, both methods of changing face can take a significant amount of time, no matter how well-trained the phalanx, and an enemy is not going to sit and wait for the phalanx to change facing. The very purpose of attacking at the flank and rear is to expose the phalanx at its vulnerable points before it can change to face the enemy. So although the sarissa phalanx had much greater frontal offensive advantages than a hoplite one and over other infantry or cavalry forces, on an extended battlefield the phalanx could prove to be a liability if its vulnerabilities were exposed.

Length of Hellenistic Sarissas

The Macedonian successes of Philip II and Alexander had been against armies that did not employ sarissas. After Alexander created his empire and introduced Macedonian-style warfare throughout, in the Eastern

Mediterranean and Asia Minor almost every army of the next two centuries utilized the sarissa phalanx. This meant that each individual sarissa phalanx no longer enjoyed a reach advantage over the enemy. As soon as every army fielded the same type of phalanx, generals were forced to seek other advantages.

For some that was in more experienced veteran phalanxes able to break enemy phalanxes consisting of new recruits. This was especially true in the period immediately following Alexander the Great's death. Then the now-famous unit of Silver Shields, veterans of Philip's and Alexander's campaigns, proved unbeatable on the battlefield in every single instance, even when outnumbered.[12] However, as generations changed, generals had to create their own veteran units from waging wars and this left each state on a level playing field.

Instead, it seems likely, though far from certain based on our limited evidence, that Hellenistic generals lengthened the sarissa as a means of regaining a reach advantage over the enemy.[13] This worked in theory as an extra rank of the phalanx could now attack the enemy front rank: six rather than five. However, lengthening the sarissa from 15ft under Alexander to 18 to 20ft under the later armies led to unforeseen problems of balance and flexibility. The longer the sarissa, the heavier and more unwieldy it becomes. Moreover, even with the best wood the extra length can see a significant bend in the shaft of the sarissa.[14] This bend severely limits the offensive capabilities of the weapon, and its greater weight reduces the power and number of thrusts a soldier can make before becoming exhausted. Making the sarissa heavier and longer also requires the soldier either to adjust the positioning of the two-hand grip on the shaft or to increase the weight of the counterbalancing butt spike or reduce the weight of the attacking blade.

A standard sarissa, according to the surviving sources and scholars who have tested them, has a handgrip roughly 3ft from its rear end.[15] This is the point of balance with the counterbalance of the butt spike. The extra reach gained from lengthening the sarissa is only applicable if the handgrip remains in the same place, thus gaining 3 to 4ft extra length at the attacking end of the weapon. However, doing so requires increasing the counterbalance weight and thus increasing the overall weight of the weapon itself even more. Our late Hellenistic tactical manuals provide most evidence for the sarissa in a Hellenistic phalanx. They also list in their terminology some of the evolutions made to the weapon and the phalanx throughout the Hellenistic period.[16] From this evidence, it seems that the arms race to lengthen the sarissa actually culminated in all armies reducing the sarissa back to at most 20ft because the longer lengths were too impractical.

So, despite a few forays into different-sized sarissas and more veteran phalangites, most Hellenistic armies fielded the same sarissa phalanx as each other. Therefore, on the battlefield any advantages gained had to come from the tactics used to defeat the enemy army as a whole and not just the phalanx itself. This brings us to the implementation in Hellenistic battles of combined arms warfare and its most efficient culmination of integrated warfare.[17]

Part 2: Macedonian-Style Armies

Combined Arms

The phalanx could not be at its best unless protected by other units in a system of combined arms. Therefore, Macedonian-style armies always fielded different types of units to protect the flanks of the phalanx. There is not one single example in history of a sarissa phalanx fighting on its own in battle. It had to be supported by other units that could protect its flanks and allow it to do what it excelled at: marching forward relentlessly and maintaining formation to hold and push back the enemy at that point in the line.

Combined arms is the modern name for a military practice that is as old as war itself: i.e. utilizing all varied types of unit together in combination so that different units or types of unit can benefit from the support of others. Each type of unit protects the vulnerabilities of other units, while also ensuring its own strengths affect the outcome of the battle. In modern warfare the unit types are more varied than in earlier eras. Tanks and armoured support fight alongside infantry and artillery and air support adds further to the unit variance. The navy and Special Forces also often add support to a conflict.

In early warfare, the troop types were simply infantry and cavalry (artillery did not appear regularly on an ancient battlefield until the height of the Roman Empire), but it is important to further categorize subsections of these two simple troop types. Missile troops fought very differently from non-missile units both as infantry and cavalry and so receive a separate designation in analyses of ancient armies. Similarly, units that fought in different ways gain separate categories. The most common and useful is the separation of heavy troops, those reliant primarily on close-quarter hand-to-hand combat, and light troops, those more suited to fighting at a relative distance. Heavy troops often wore more armour or had heavier weapons than lighter troops, but the main distinction is between how they fought and not what armour they wore. Some lightly-armed or armoured troops would fight in the melee and equally some heavy armoured troops preferred to fight at a distance.

So there are a number of distinct troop types in ancient armies that should be distinguished from each other in terms of their battle roles: heavy, light and missile infantry, and heavy, light and missile cavalry. These are the six basic categories. Further to this, elephants and chariots acted as heavy cavalry in battle. However, both are clearly distinct units since they could also function as missile-only units and had their own peculiar advantages and disadvantages. Additionally, at Magnesia camel-riders acted as missile cavalry, but clearly in view of their lack of speed and manoeuvrability we should class them separately from horse-archers. Missile troops often fought separately as javelin men, slingers and archers. Generals usually brigaded each type of missile unit separately since each had different strengths and weaknesses.

Finally, some cultures fought more like medium infantry halfway between heavy and light. These units usually wore little armour and so could move faster, and could fight at range since they often fought with javelins or lighter spears they were able to throw, but they were equally adept at fighting at close quarters in the hand-to-hand melee. In the ancient world, the best examples of this are Celtic warrior bands that had virtually no armour at all but fought fiercely in the melee. So we can create a list of the various unit types listing their name, armour, armament and battle role:

Unit Type	Armour	Armament	Traditional Battle Roles
Heavy infantry	Strong body armour, shield and helmet	Various. In Classical or Hellenistic Greek warfare either spears or sarissas with a short sword for close-quarter defence	Close-quarter combat in the thick of the melee
Medium infantry	Some light body armour, usually a helmet, a shield (usually, though they could use a two-handed melee weapon instead)	Swords, axes, spears, clubs or other melee weapon of one or two hands	Close-quarter combat in the melee but could throw spears if necessary
Light infantry (peltasts in Greek terminology)	Some body armour, usually a helmet, often some kind of shield	Usually a spear, sometimes javelins (peltasts), and for close quarters a small sword, axe or other cutting blade	Against cavalry or missile troops or at the edge of the melee but can fight at close quarters if needed, though not against heavy infantry
Javelin men	Some body armour, usually a helmet, often some kind of shield	Javelins and a secondary defensive cutting blade	Ranged attack
Archers	Rarely any armour (though some cultures had heavy armoured archers), sometimes a helmet	Bow and a secondary defensive cutting blade	Ranged attack
Slingers	No armour usually	Sling and stone or lead sling-stones or bullets and a secondary defensive cutting blade	Ranged attack
Heavy cavalry	Strong body armour, shield and helmet	Usually a spear or lance and a sword	Charging into close-quarter combat
Light cavalry (usually javelin-armed cavalry mirroring the javelin infantry)	Some body armour, usually a helmet, often some kind of shield	Usually a javelin or spear and sword, but sometimes a lance	Range fighting at the edge of the melee but can fight at close quarters if needed

Unit Type	Armour	Armament	Traditional Battle Roles
Javelin-armed ranged cavalry (the term Tarantine cavalry)	Some body armour, usually a helmet, often some kind of shield	Always a javelin but could use a spear and sword if attacked and forced to fight hand-to-hand	Always engaged in ranged fighting at the edge of the melee; some units rode in a continuous circle throwing javelins at the enemy and moving just out of the enemy's range when needed
Horse-archers	Some armour	Bow and a sword	Ranged attack
Elephants	Animals had defensive towers and perhaps some armour. Riders (mahouts) often wore armour	Riders used javelins and bows	Mainly ranged attack but could charge into the melee if needed. Often charged indiscriminately if wounded or scared
Scythed chariots	Defensive armour for drivers and sometimes horses	Riders used javelins and bows, scythes on the wheels or chariot	Ranged and to charge into a disordered enemy line; better used for pursuit
Camel-archers	Some armour	Bow and a sword	Ranged attack

In addition, to properly understand combined arms and how the units go together, we can separate our list into a handy table that includes the strengths and weaknesses of each unit type as well as where they usually fought in a battle line:

Unit Type	Strengths	Weaknesses	Usual Battle Position
Heavy infantry	Excellent in close combat	Phalanx weak on flanks and rear, slow to change positions	Centre of the battle line
Medium infantry	Good in close combat, very manoeuvrable	Lack of armour made them vulnerable to heavier units	On the edges of the centre to protect the flanks of the heavy infantry
Light infantry	Very manoeuvrable, can perform different roles, link between cavalry and infantry	No formation, exposed in close combat or to cavalry charge	On the flanks of the other heavier infantry, to hold rough terrain, and link to cavalry, often stationed between elephants
Javelin men	Missile barrage can penetrate well at close range, can overcome cavalry, chariots and elephants	No formation, exposed in close combat or to heavy cavalry charge	On the flanks of the other infantry, to hold rough terrain and link to cavalry, or to skirmish in front of the whole battle line, often stationed between elephants
Archers	Can fire missiles rapidly over a good distance	Very weak in close combat. Some states fielded armoured archers to improve their defence at close quarters	On the flanks of the other infantry, or to skirmish in front of the whole battle line
Slingers	Can fire missiles rapidly over a good distance, more penetration of missiles than other ranged units	Very weak in close combat	On the flanks of the other infantry, or to skirmish in front of the whole battle line
Heavy cavalry	Excellent in close combat, devastating charge	Vulnerable to infantry if static, slower than other cavalry to change positions	On the wings from whence to launch a devastating charge, but not on the very edge
Light cavalry (not javelin-armed)	Pursuing fleeing enemy, skirmishing, scouting, linking to heavy cavalry	Vulnerable in close combat	On the edge of the wings of the army as a flank guard, also to connect infantry and cavalry

Unit Type	Strengths	Weaknesses	Usual Battle Position
Javelin cavalry	Ranged missile attack often while wheeling in a circle in front of or on the flanks of the enemy, skirmishing	Vulnerable in close combat	On the edge of the wings of the army with space to wheel in a circle, or attack and withdraw in traditional skirmishing tactics
Horse-archers	Can fire missiles rapidly over a long distance, some can wheel in front of enemy	Vulnerable in close combat	Skirmishing on the wings
Elephants	Defensively strong in size and space, terrifying to troops and horses not used to them, can fire missiles over the infantry, charge can be devastating if harnessed correctly	Animals vulnerable to missiles, tender feet vulnerable to spikes in the ground, can run amok and cause damage to friendly soldiers if goaded, injured, the driver is killed or the lead elephant dies	Defensive positions on the wings in front of the other troops, sometimes in the front of the whole line, held back at an angle as flank defence
Scythed chariots	Devastating charge against disordered or fleeing enemy cavalry or infantry	Horses too vulnerable to missiles, can run amok into friendly forces if horses are driverless, scared or wounded	On the flanks or the front of an army with the space to charge, best held back in reserve to launch on a fleeing or disorganized enemy
Camel-archers	Good missile range, camels can scare horses unused to them	Very slow and can scare friendly horses	In the wings alongside other light cavalry

Phalanxes usually occupied the centre of the battle line since they took up so much more space than light infantry or cavalry and could pin the enemy in one place. A 16,000-strong sarissa phalanx, the usual Hellenistic deployment strength, occupied a large amount of ground. Philip II, in the first known uses of the sarissa phalanx in battle, used light infantry to protect one flank and heavy cavalry on the other.[18] Alexander the Great used the same basic methods except that he commanded so many more and different types of unit. He added different types of light and heavy infantry on both flanks of the phalanx, and stationed light, missile and heavy cavalry on both his wings. That way the sarissa phalanx in the centre was directly shielded by other infantry that marched at a slightly faster speed. This also prevented the phalanx from being left behind and gaps forming between the different units in the battle line that advanced at a faster pace. The cavalry units, which required more space in which to operate, could wheel and charge on the open wings of the whole army without their rapid charge exposing the flanks of the phalanx to attack.

The Hellenistic armies, which as standard also employed elephants, added these large animals as a further means of flank defence for the phalanx. Elephants could also charge or threaten to charge the enemy flank and phalanx. Usually light infantry stood next to or intermingled with the elephants in case the elephants did have to charge. These light infantry troops then filled in as the phalanx's flank defence.

However, the large elephants had their disadvantages that often outweighed the benefits. Elephants are herd animals so they follow their leader. If the lead animal died, lost its driver (mahout) or retreated, most often the rest of the herd also ran away. Sarissas, javelins, arrows, axes and caltrops (spikes in the ground) often could harass the elephants enough to persuade them to turn around. More often than not elephants in distress in battle will run amok and be just as likely to turn on their own side as on the enemy. A number of battles changed from victory to defeat because a defensive elephant alignment went irretrievably awry.[19]

Other than elephants, only a few other unit types appeared in Macedonian-style armies after Alexander, such as cataphracts, camels and scythed chariots. The most interesting of these new unit types is the cataphract. A unit of very heavy cavalry where the rider and horse both wore heavy armour, cataphracts would launch devastating charges into enemy ranks much like medieval knights.[20] Alexander did encounter the forerunners of these cavalry units in his campaign in Bactria and Sogdiana and in the Persian army at Gaugamela, but he did not field them in his own army. Antiochus fielded 3,000 cataphracts at Magnesia, but not with the effect that they should have achieved.

So, regardless of the specific ethnicity, armament and style of the units in an army, combined arms gets the most out of every single one. Macedonian-style armies of the fourth century perfected this use of combined arms into a simple formula: sarissa phalanx of 12,000-16,000 in the centre often split into two wings; elite veteran mobile heavy infantry (often hoplites or hypaspists) on the right or both of the immediate flanks of the phalanx; mobile light infantry (usually archers and javelin men) as the infantry flank guards especially on the left; heavy cavalry on one or both wings ready to charge the enemy at speed; and finally light cavalry on the very edges of the army line. Elephants, if available, would protect one or both flanks as well as sometimes the centre. Also, if available, armies would have a unit called hamippoi, which were elite infantry whose sole job was to run beside the heavy cavalry and fight on foot alongside them as melee defence while also maintaining a connection to the slower-moving infantry in the centre.[21]

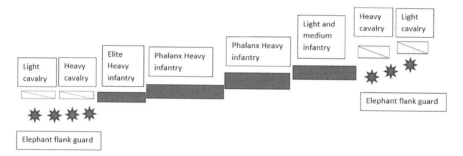

Figure 1. Standard Macedonian-style army deployment.

This standard deployment in Macedonian armies meant that the generals and soldiers always knew what their role was. However, it also meant that when fighting other Macedonian armies the deployment was often identical. Victory then came down to whoever made the best tactical use of their army units in combined arms.

Hammer and Anvil

The main way that combined arms worked in conjunction with the phalanx is commonly referred to as the hammer and anvil tactic. The large, slow and impenetrable sarissa phalanx in the centre acted as the solid anvil, while other more mobile units attacked elsewhere as the hammer. These hammer units, usually cavalry because of their greater speed and offensive power in a charge, tried to turn the enemy soldiers towards the smashing power of the oncoming phalanx anvil and trap them in between. The attacks could come from either wing or both. This is the famous 'horns of the buffalo' tactic used in other eras and cultures to surround the enemy and push them into the centre. The most successful uses in history are arguably by Hannibal at Cannae against the Romans and the Zulus at Isandlwana against the British.[22] Macedonian-style armies rarely utilized the double envelopment since it was more important to refuse the one flank to prevent disaster, as discussed below.

Though the term hammer and anvil does apply, rarely did the cavalry hammer attack actually push the enemy back onto the phalanx anvil. Rather, the cavalry more often than not simply broke the will of the enemy and precipitated a complete rout of the entire enemy line. Iphicrates' famous body part metaphor, as quoted by Plutarch (*Pelopidas* 2.1), provides very useful imagery to better understand the system: 'as Iphicrates analyzed the matter, the light-armed troops are like the hands, the cavalry like the feet, the phalanx itself like the chest and breast plate, and the general like the head.' In the more nuanced terms of a kick-boxer, with heavy cavalry rather than just the light cavalry only familiar to Iphicrates, the phalanx acts as the body of the battle line and the cavalry as the fists or feet delivering the knockout blow.[23]

Part 3: Standard Macedonian Battle Tactics

Refused Flank
Pioneered by Philip II of Macedon, likely as a necessary component of waging battle with a sarissa phalanx, the principal Macedonian battle tactic was the refused flank. This process involved drawing up the battle line at an angle so that one wing was significantly more advanced than the other. In most battles, the right wing advanced and the left held back. This tactic served a number of crucial purposes in aiding the use of combined arms and the phalanx in particular.

Both flanks of the phalanx as well as its rear are very vulnerable as discussed above. By holding one wing back, the line extends so far as to gain significant time for the phalanx to advance slowly in the centre before a stronger enemy wing could get around and attack the flank or rear. It also allows the phalanx itself to deploy at an angle with each separate regiment within the whole phalanx held back slightly behind the other to its right. The rightmost regiment has its right flank protected by the flank guard of other, usually elite heavy infantry and it protects the

xxvi   The Battles of Antiochus the Great

right flank of the next regiment. This one in turn protects the flank of the regiment to its left and so on down the line. It is not clear from the sources exactly how far behind each other the regiments deployed, but that likely varied depending on the circumstances. In Alexander's army, there were six regiments each under the command of an eponymous general from whom the regiment gained its name and who probably commanded his troops on horseback from the rear of the formation.[24] Later Hellenistic armies deployed more and different sized regiments, but the deployment remained the same style.

By refusing the left flank, a general knew that the battle-defining attack would take place on the right wing. As a result, any commander would place his best units on the right wing since they would do most of the fighting. The left wing guard featured the next strongest cavalry units in the army, which were best suited to defend the expected enemy attack. In Alexander's army his assault force on the right wing was always his elite Companion cavalry, and his left wing strength was in his Thessalian cavalry, which was just as good.

The advanced right wing always determined to charge the enemy. This was where the variance in tactics came in. The assault always came from heavy cavalry, but the target of the assault had to be carefully chosen. The most successful charges came against gaps in the enemy line. To find one of those, a general often had to create one by other tactics. The best example in all military history is Alexander the Great's manoeuvre at Gaugamela. Outnumbered almost five to one, Alexander had to attack even faster than usual to win the victory before the superior numbers of the Persians enveloped his refused wing. Since he had used the same deployment at the prior Battle of Issus, the Persians knew what to expect. Therefore, Alexander sent a sacrificial unit of light infantry and cavalry out in front of his right wing. This is similar to his method innovated at the Granicus.[25] This small force drew the Persian left-wing cavalry into an attack, and the speed of their attack left a gap in the rest of the Persian line. Alexander personally led the assault through the gap and caused such instant carnage that the entire Persian army retreated.[26]

In every Macedonian-style battle the commanding generals had to find a way to ensure that their right-wing charge was more effective and devastating to the enemy than the one the enemy launched in response at the refused left flank. This game of cat and mouse and the natural variance in comparative abilities of units and generals is what usually decided the victor and the loser.

In some Hellenistic battles, notably at Gabiene and also at Raphia as discussed in Chapter 2, generals sometimes chose to oppose the enemy's strike cavalry force with their own. This saw both sides refusing their wing on the same side of the battlefield, one army's right and one's left. As at Raphia, as discussed below, this method of meeting the enemy head-on depended on which army had the best cavalry or, as shown by Antigonus at Gabiene, which general was best able to take advantage of unexpected battlefield conditions determined the outcome. At Gabiene, Eumenes decided to face Antigonus' strike cavalry head-on since he had failed to win at Paraetacene earlier using the normal tactic. It backfired when the cloud of dust raised by the initial skirmishing allowed Antigonus to surprise Eumenes with a flanking cavalry attack. Eumenes' elite cavalry fled instead of meeting the enemy head-on as he had intended.[27]

Without a defensively refused wing, the phalanx and the whole battle line was vulnerable. The success of an enemy charge depended on turning the flank and getting in behind to attack the vulnerabilities of sarissa phalangites before the slow advance of the phalanx had caused enough damage of its own in the centre. Eumenes of Cardia, one of the greatest commanders after Alexander the Great, only salvaged a draw from defeat at Paraetacene when Antigonus' heavy cavalry overcame his left wing because the enemy cavalry was far enough away to allow his superior phalanx time to prevail in the centre (Diodorus 19.26-31). As we shall see in this book, Antiochus' main mistakes that led to his defeat at Magnesia was not refusing his left wing and not returning from pursuit in time to aid the phalanx in the centre. This latter problem also cost him victory at the Battle of Raphia.

Feigned Withdrawal

Another tactic that became standard in Macedonian-style armies but was not as necessary for victory in every engagement was the feigned withdrawal. Again, Philip II first used it at Chaeronea. At this battle the Greek hoplites thought the Macedonians were retreating up a hill and so charged out of their own phalanx formation only to come unstuck upon the devastating downward charge of a still organized sarissa phalanx. The success of the tactic prompted its use elsewhere. Alexander may have even used the tactic during a siege at both Thebes and Halicarnassus as a way to draw the defenders out of the safety of their ramparts and into a killing zone of the waiting heavy infantry.[28]

The feigned withdrawal almost certainly won the Battle of Ipsus for the allied army against Antigonus when Seleucus' son, the future Antiochus I, retreated with his heavy cavalry on the left wing to draw away Demetrius' victorious Antigonid heavy cavalry. Seleucus then deployed a reserve of more than 400 elephants to plug the gap and prevent Demetrius' return to the battlefield.[29] Since the Antigonid army had no other cavalry to shield the phalanx in the centre, the victory was a foregone conclusion for the allies (Plutarch, *Demetrius* 28-29; Appian, *Syrian Wars* 55). Perhaps because of Seleucus' success at Ipsus, the Seleucid army used this same tactic on numerous occasions; especially, it seems, in the Jewish wars.[30]

Summary

Thus there were many ways to make the most of a sarissa phalanx in battle, but they all relied on fielding different types of units in different roles and employing the best use of combined arms. As long as the terrain was suitable to maintain an unbroken front rank, or the soldiers experienced enough to fight on uneven terrain and other units shielded the vulnerable flanks and rear using suitable and proven tactics, the sarissa phalanx was virtually unassailable in the centre of a battle. This was the way of war in the Eastern Mediterranean for almost 200 years until the arrival of Rome.

Alexander the Great still stands as the finest proponent of winning battles using the sarissa phalanx, heavy cavalry and combined arms. Alexander's greatest strength as a general was in knowing how to utilize each different type of unit correctly in an overall battle plan. This is the culmination of the theory of combined arms: getting the best use out of each distinct unit in an army to defend other units or to attack the enemy, safe in the knowledge that its own shortcomings are nullified. This apex point of perfect combined arms usage I call integrated warfare. In all Alexander's battles he used the same tactics and relied on the same units with only minimal variation. It was this consistency in application of tactics that allowed the Macedonian army to become so efficient and successful in battle.

Unfortunately, after the wars of the Successors, the expertise fell away in subsequent generations so that by the time of the Roman arrival in the Mediterranean Macedonian-style armies were nowhere near as efficient or able as those of the late fourth century. Defeat after defeat to the Roman legion style of warfare suggests an innate superiority over the sarissa phalanx. However, that superiority is only over poorly-trained and inexperienced phalanxes deployed in an army that inadequately used combined arms, as in the case of almost all late Hellenistic ones.

The armies of Philip II, Alexander and the Successors were unquestionably superior to later ones, so much so that we should draw a clear distinction between the key periods of Macedonian-style warfare. Battles up to the end of the Successors all showed the perfect use of combined arms in armies that fielded expertly-led, trained and experienced phalanxes and heavy cavalry. The first unit cannot function best in a battle without the other.

After Seleucus defeated Lysimachus at Corupedium in 281 and Pyrrhus died in defeat against Argos in 275, the generation of generals schooled under Alexander ended. The next phase of generalship, from 275 until the arrival of Rome in 198, saw numerous battles between Macedonian-style armies but no clear standout generals other than Philopoemen, whose successes will be discussed later. Similar armies fought against each other and the victory usually depended on whose troops fought better or, sometimes, who led the best. More importantly, this period saw a decline in the expertise of sarissa phalanxes and a reduction in the number and quality of heavy cavalry deployed alongside them.

From the victory of Rome over a Macedonian-style army, at Aous in 198 and Cynoscephalae in 197, until the final Roman defeat of the last Macedonian-style army of Pontus in 47 BCE, the Roman military style was unquestionably superior. However, this does not make the Roman legion inherently superior over all sarissa phalanx-focused armies. It is impossible to compare eras. Certainly, engaged as they were with regional conflicts, the Roman army of the 330s would not match the experienced armies of Alexander, but the later Roman legions of the late Republic and early Empire, expertly led and experienced in constant warfare, may well have overcome the earlier Macedonian armies. This comparison is one that always enthuses military historians and fans but is without answer. Suffice to examine here in this book that the later Macedonian-style armies, including those of Antiochus III, were pale shades compared with the armies that repeatedly conquered and reconquered Greece, Asia Minor, Mesopotamia and Egypt in the fourth century. I argue that the phalanx as part of a combined arms system was not inherently inferior to the Roman way of war as Polybius and Roman historians would have us believe. Rather, the phalanxes and Macedonian-style armies that fought Rome in the second and first centuries BCE were led and organized so badly that they nullified the strengths of the Macedonian-style army and left the weaknesses exposed to the Romans' benefit.

Chapter One

The Seleucid Army of Antiochus the Great

To understand the make-up of the Seleucid army of Antiochus III, it is important to briefly outline the origins of the Seleucid Empire and its manpower resources. Seleucus Nicator had founded the Seleucid Empire with the help of Ptolemy I Soter of Egypt. At the Treaty of Triparadeisos, probably in 321 BCE, Antipater, the Macedonian governor of Alexander the Great's Empire, had initially appointed Seleucus as governor of Babylon. However, in 315 Antigonus Monophthalmus, the strongest of Alexander the Great's Successor generals, while staying in Babylon fell out with Seleucus and then tried to remove him from office. Seleucus fled to Egypt for support and with the help of Ptolemy reinstalled himself in Babylon in 312. He then spent the next fifteen years taking control of the other Macedonian-ruled satrapies and provinces in the east.

Twice Antigonus sent an army to oust Seleucus in 312 and 311 BCE. The first army of 17,000 men Seleucus ambushed with an army of only 3,000 and took over the soldiers of the enemy. This one act established his rule in Babylon and gave him the army to conquer the neighbouring regions. The second army of Antigonus was commanded by his son Demetrius, but Seleucus' power grew too fast and he easily maintained his control. Finally, in 311 or 310 Antigonus invaded at the head of an army of 80,000 men. Unfortunately, our sources for this war are exclusively a somewhat unreliable account by Polyaenus (Polyaenus, 4.9.1) of a decisive battle won by Seleucus through a clever stratagem and a very vague summary in the *Babylonian Chronicle*. We have no details at all about the make-up of Seleucus' army, which is our interest here; just that he had enough troops to defeat Antigonus' large invasion.

Seleucus, established in Mesopotamia, then made war on the great Indian king Chandragupta, who founded the long-lasting Mauryan dynasty. Seleucus' aims for the campaign and the army he took do not survive. Our few surviving sources both in Greek and Indian traditions suggest that he crossed the Indus but Chandragupta either defeated him or fought to a stalemate. Whatever happened militarily, the result was a treaty between the two kings that saw Seleucus cede control of probably four provinces on the western side of the Indus in return for 500 elephants and probably a marriage alliance of Seleucus' daughter to Chandragupta or his son. The other rival Hellenistic kings satirize Seleucus as the Elephant General for giving away so much territory for such a minimal return.[1] One critical rumour suggests that the 500 elephants were all male, also thus preventing Seleucus from establishing a breeding programme. Nonetheless, the 500 elephants proved to be militarily very decisive in the battles that followed.

Eventually, after a decade of infighting and territorial changes, all the Hellenistic kings together (Seleucus I of Babylon, Ptolemy I of Egypt, Cassander of Macedon and Lysimachus of Thrace) allied against Antigonus and his son Demetrius. Seleucus was chiefly responsible for the final allied victory over Antigonus at the famous Battle of Ipsus in 301 BCE largely because of his clever use of an elephant reserve to block the return of Demetrius' victorious cavalry. This feigned withdrawal of Seleucid cavalry led by his son Antiochus I, as discussed above, became a standard Seleucid battle tactic. Seleucus' own ambitions to create an empire to rival Alexander the Great's ended in his murder shortly after his victorious battle with Lysimachus at Corupedium in 281 BCE (Appian, *Syrian Wars*, 62).

Later Seleucid kings established their authority over all the provinces from Asia Minor to India despite a few rebellions from time to time. The biggest threat to Seleucid power was the invasion in 245 BCE of Ptolemy III Euergetes. Instigated to aid Ptolemy's sister Berenice, the ousted second wife of the recently deceased Antiochus II, her death prompted an all-out invasion of the empire. Though the sources are not detailed, Appian states that Ptolemy's invasion advanced to Babylon and the *Babylonian Chronicle* states that he took all of the city of Babylon except for the palace, which held out for a long time.[2] He also, perhaps more importantly, captured the city of Seleucia Pieria, the port city of the Seleucid western capital Antioch, and left a garrison there, which remained until the start of Antiochus III's invasion of Syria in 219. Ptolemy was on the verge of complete victory when apparent unrest back in Egypt forced his withdrawal.

Though we know little about the exact units in the early armies of the Seleucid kings, the one advantage all the Seleucid kings enjoyed over other Macedonian descendant monarchs was access to thousands of troops of all varieties and ethnicities in Asia. Despite Seleucus I's sale of four eastern provinces to Chandragupta for 500 elephants, the Seleucid army could still call on vast numbers of soldiers and every troop type in the Hellenistic world. Certainly elephants featured prominently in the major battles of Seleucus I and also of his son Antiochus I.

The *Babylonian Chronicle* describes elephants from Bactria mustering in Babylon before or just after Seleucus headed out on his fateful campaign against Lysimachus.[3] Antiochus I is famous both now and at the time for his so-called elephant victory over the invading Galatians in Asia Minor. There is no clear evidence for exactly what army he deployed or how many elephants. Lucian in the *Antiochus* states sixteen, but this is likely part of his satirical battle narrative that alters troop numbers to make his point. The only slightly more reliable *Suda* states that Antiochus won when his elephants overcame the Galatian cavalry.[4] We know that the Seleucids developed a limited elephant-breeding programme at Apamea. Presumably over the years they also received more elephants through good relations with the Mauryan dynasty in India as Antiochus III did later. Elephants were a regular feature on Seleucid coins from Seleucus I onwards likely demonstrating regal majesty,[5] but no doubt also a connection to Seleucus' now famous 500 Indian elephants and their vital role at the empire-making Battle of Ipsus.

The only evidence we have for any troop totals or unit breakdown for a Seleucid army before Antiochus III is for Seleucus' contingent at the Battle of Ipsus in 301 BCE. Diodorus states that Seleucus brought 20,000 infantry, 12,000 cavalry including horse-archers, 480 elephants and more than 100 scythed chariots (Diodorus 20.113). The infantry probably consisted of sarissa phalanx and light troops. A previous engagement with Antigonus had removed around 20 elephants from Seleucus' 500.[6] Plutarch lists 120 scythed chariots (Plutarch, *Demetrius* 28). The cavalry total of Diodorus is more than the 10,500 total given by Plutarch for the whole allied army, so it is not clear exactly how many Seleucus did bring.

Nevertheless, even with this brief description we can already see the standard units of the Seleucid army: infantry including the sarissa phalanx and light troops, elephants, cavalry including heavy cavalry and horse-archers and scythed chariots. The chariots were a Persian tradition utilized in number by Darius III in the Battle of Gaugamela against Alexander the Great. Antiochus III also used them in his battles, but they were not very useful faced with anti-chariot tactics and a sarissa phalanx. Seleucid armies very much resembled all other Hellenistic Macedonian-style combined arms armies, with the addition of scythed chariots.

Unfortunately, we do not have much information on the exact organization and specific unit make-up of the earliest Seleucid armies in the third century, but they cannot have been very different from the armies of Antiochus III at the end of the century, for which there is evidence. This is the timeframe of concern here and so this chapter will examine the units and standard battle tactics and deployments for Antiochus' various battles.

Antiochus' army must have been very much like the army of his predecessors. He came to the throne as a teenager unexpectedly and leaned on advisors for his first campaigns. Polybius provides the details of the first army Antiochus led into battle at Apollonia against the rebellious forces of Molon, the satrap of Media. Polybius (Polybius, *Histories* 5.53) describes it as such:

> On his right wing he posted first his lancers under the command of Ardys, an officer of proved ability in the field, next them the Cretan allies and next them the Gallic Rhigosages. After these he placed the mercenaries from Greece and last of all the phalanx. The left wing he assigned to the cavalry known as 'Companions'. His elephants, which were ten in number, he posted at certain intervals in front of the line. He distributed his reserves of infantry and cavalry between the two wings with orders to outflank the enemy as soon as the battle had begun.[7]

So we can see how Antiochus' army mirrored the standard Hellenistic deployment of phalanx in the centre, other infantry on its direct flanks and heavy strike cavalry on both wings. Elephants and other infantry added extra protection in front of his wings (presumably rather than in front of the phalanx; Polybius does not specify) and on this occasion kept others on the flanks as reserves.

Before his invasion of Egypt he had no time, experience or need to reform his army's recruitment or organization and so it must have featured much of the same army as against Molon. Polybius (5.79), as is often the case for this period, gives the fullest account of Antiochus' forces at Raphia:

These consisted first of Daae, Carmanians and Cilicians, light-armed troops about five thousand in number organized and commanded by Byttacus the Macedonian. Under Theodotus the Aetolian, who had played the traitor to Ptolemy, was a force of ten thousand selected from every part of the kingdom and armed in the Macedonian manner, most of them with silver shields. The phalanx was about twenty thousand strong and was under the command of Nicarchus and Theodotus surnamed Hemiolius. There were Agrianian and Persian bowmen and slingers to the number of two thousand, and with them two thousand Thracians, all under the command of Menedemus of Alabanda. Aspasianus the Mede had under him a force of about five thousand Medes, Cissians, Cadusians and Carmanians. The Arabs and neighbouring tribes numbered about ten thousand and were commanded by Zabdibelus. Hippolochus the Thessalian commanded the mercenaries from Greece, five thousand in number. Antiochus had also fifteen hundred Cretans under Eurylochus and a thousand Neocretans under Zelys of Gortyna. With these were five hundred Lydian javelineers and a thousand Cardaces under Lysimachus the Gaul. The cavalry numbered six thousand in all, four thousand of them being commanded by Antipater the king's nephew and the rest by Themison. The whole army of Antiochus consisted of sixty-two thousand foot, six thousand horse and a hundred and two elephants.

In total he had the following:

30,000 sarissa phalangites

5,000 Greek mercenaries, most likely hoplites

20,000 light infantry (not missile)

8,000 missile infantry, bowmen and javelin men

6,000 cavalry in two units: one of 4,000 commanded by Antiochus' nephew and likely royal heavy cavalry, and one of 2,000 probably light cavalry

102 elephants

This force collected by Antiochus from throughout his empire and alliances clearly has a huge emphasis on infantry. It is a ratio of infantry to cavalry of 10:1. This is roughly the standard size of most Hellenistic armies after Ipsus.

However, in the successful era-defining armies of Philip II and Alexander the Great the ratio was much closer. Alexander led 40,000 infantry and 7,000 cavalry for a ratio of 7:1. Since the use of combined arms with the sarissa phalanx is so reliant on cavalry support, this ratio is crucial to understand the efficiency of an army. Alexander led 12,000 phalangites and hypaspists, his elite infantry guard regiment. The ratio of phalanx to cavalry was 2:1. Antiochus' phalanx to cavalry ratio was 5:1. That is a significant difference that would substantially increase the importance of the cavalry as a shield of the vulnerabilities of the phalanx. However, it is similar to the ratios of standard Hellenistic armies of Alexander's Successors.

The Battles of Paraitacene and Gabiene are good examples of the standard ratio of phalanx to (all) cavalry in Macedonian-style armies of the late fourth century.[8] These two battles witnessed epic confrontations of the two best generals of Alexander's Successors, Antigonus Monophthalmus and Eumenes of Cardia. Both generals enjoyed a ratio of phalanx infantry to cavalry of 3:1. Antigonus had 28,000 men in the phalanx, but most were raw recruits. He had 4,000 heavy cavalry and another 6,000 light cavalry to provide his offensive thrust on the flanks. Eumenes had a veteran phalanx of 17,000 and 6,000 cavalry.

The Battle of Ipsus reinforces the ratio of phalanx to cavalry. At Ipsus, Antigonus had 45,000 heavy infantry and 10,000 cavalry, a ratio of 4.5:1 and his enemy had 40,000 heavy infantry and 15,000 cavalry, a ratio of 3:1. In fact, Seleucus' contribution to the allied army, as discussed above, featured 20,000 phalanx infantry and 12,000 cavalry. That is fewer than 2:1, an almost exact mirror of the ratio seen in Alexander's army. Clearly, at the end of the fourth century Alexander's Successors appreciated the value of such a strong force of cavalry to support and complement the sarissa phalanx on the battlefield. In fact, such a strong force of cavalry was almost imperative for the best functioning of combined arms on the sarissa phalanx-centred battlefield.

Antiochus, as demonstrated by his later army totals, could have called on more cavalry. At a council in Achaea, where Antiochus' representatives along with the Aetolians attempted to persuade the Achaeans to join in the war on Rome in the build-up to the battles of Thermopylae and Magnesia, his ambassadors emphasized the size and nature of Antiochus' cavalry force. The envoys even went so far as to state that '[E]ven if the armies of the whole of Europe were brought together, they would be crushed by these cavalry forces' (Livy 35.48.4), demonstrating that Antiochus' strength lay in his cavalry. This is undoubtedly exaggeration since at Magnesia Antiochus fielded only 12,000 cavalry, hardly enough to crush all the forces of Europe, but this is still twice the number at Raphia. As we shall see in the following chapter, this lack of cavalry at Raphia came to be a thorn in his side. For whatever reason, and this is perhaps the crucial question in trying to understand Antiochus' underachievement as a general, he did not field massive numbers of cavalry against other Hellenistic-style armies or the Romans.

Though we have no detailed descriptions of Antiochus' other battles until Magnesia, Polybius (16.18), in his criticism of Zeno's account of the Battle of Panion, does provide a vague list of unit types. He states:

> Antiochus, he [Zeno] says, had at early dawn sent off his elder son, Antiochus, with a portion of his forces to occupy the parts of the hill which commanded the enemy, and when it was daylight he took the rest of his army across the river which separated the two camps and drew it up on the plain, placing the phalanx in one line opposite the enemy's centre and stationing some of his cavalry to the left of the phalanx and some to the right, among the latter being the troop of mailed horsemen which was all under the command of his younger son, Antiochus. Next he tells us that the king posted the elephants at some distance in advance of the phalanx together with Antipater's Tarantines, the spaces between the elephants being filled with bowmen and slingers, while he himself with his horse and foot guards took up a position behind the elephants.

From this we can see that Antiochus' army again featured a strong phalanx in the centre, with the usual deployment of light infantry on the flanks and heavy cavalry on the wings with light cavalry on the furthest extremities of each wing. Also elephants fronted each wing with light infantry stationed between them. Polybius actually criticizes Zeno's account for suggesting that elephants were stationed in front of the phalanx but then the two phalanxes engaged each other without stating what happened to the elephants. We will examine this battle in more detail in Chapter 3 and correct Polybius' misunderstandings. In this battle the Seleucids also fielded a unit of mailed cavalry better known as cataphracts. These heavy cavalry, the forerunners of medieval mailed knights, predominantly came from Bactria. Antiochus III had just returned from an expedition to subdue that region before he invaded Syria and fought at Panion. This cavalry unit featured importantly in the Battle of Magnesia as we shall see later.

Nonetheless, in all Antiochus' battles, his army's total strength and its basic organization mirrored the standard Macedonian-style combined arms army. Antiochus marshalled his army in the standard Macedonian-style deployment as discussed above: a core of a sarissa phalanx in the centre of the battle line supported with light infantry on each of its flanks and cavalry, fronted by elephants, on the extreme of each wing. Incidentally, the Egyptian armies at Raphia and Panion drew up opposite Antiochus in the same way, as was the traditional Hellenistic deployment of the previous 130 years.

At Magnesia Antiochus fielded the most diverse Macedonian-style army for decades. Though probably smaller than his army at Raphia, it featured different units. Perhaps this was one of Antiochus' difficulties, but we shall discuss that in detail later. Here it is enough to confirm the different types of unit in Antiochus' army rather than the specific ethnicities.

If we trust our sources, Antiochus' army had the standard 16,000-strong sarissa phalanx and elite heavy cavalry. He also commanded Gallic infantry. This unit I categorize as medium infantry in the tables in the introduction because it is not clear if they wore much armour. They certainly expected culturally to fight in the melee in hand-to-hand combat. He had slingers, archers and javelin men from many different areas as well as other light infantry or peltasts. For cavalry he had light and missile troops of various types. He also had a contingent of cataphracts from Galatia as mail-clad super-heavy cavalry. He commanded scythed chariots and elephants and one small unit of camel-archers.

Thus Antiochus in all his battles benefited from calling upon every type of unit possible and incorporating them into his battle line but not his battle plan, the crucial element of combined arms. Diverse in type does not mean combined. Macedonian-style armies relied on a complete integration of every type of unit in the army to benefit each other. Perhaps the sheer numbers of languages and nationalities in Antiochus' army prevented that. Whatever the reason, Antiochus never really got the best use out of all the units in his army, unfortunately, as we shall see.

Tactics

The principal standard tactics of Macedonian-style armies were the withheld flank and the hammer and anvil. At Raphia, Antiochus drew up his forces as expected but added a unit of light cavalry on his right wing at an angle to prevent the enemy cavalry outflanking his own cavalry force. His left wing was enlarged by the addition of the majority of his 20,000 light infantry and elephants, but our sources do not say specifically that he held the wing back at an angle. This is the most crucial piece of tactical information. The Macedonian battle tactics perfected by Philip II and Alexander relied almost entirely on a withheld left wing, en echelon as the formation is known. This tactical device delivered the crucial extra time for the right-wing cavalry to charge into the enemy wing. This is the connection to the other tactic, the hammer and anvil. The charge of the right-wing cavalry was intended to win the battle as the hammer and drive the enemy towards the centre and into the waiting sarissas of the phalanx as the anvil.

Against Molon, at the very start of the battle, the rebels' left wing simply switched sides to fight for Antiochus and so we have no idea if Antiochus intended to withdraw one of his flanks. Antiochus attempted to lead a cavalry charge as a hammer onto the anvil at Raphia as discussed in the next chapter, but since he did not withdraw his left wing he denied himself the extra time he needed and he chased the enemy cavalry too far. We have no clear description of the Battle of

Panion, so it is not clear if Antiochus withdrew his left flank at this battle either. The confusing description of Polybius criticizes Zeno for having elephants on that wing scaring Aetolian cavalry into retreat. So if Zeno is correct, that wing also attacked the enemy line rather than holding back defensively. What is clear about Panion is that Antiochus' heavy cavalry charge on his right wing, led by the heavily-armoured cataphracts, completely routed the enemy cavalry and light infantry and exposed the vulnerabilities of the phalanx. It was the arrival of that cavalry force returning to the battlefield that prompted the Egyptian commander to withdraw.

Zeno also suggests that the Seleucid phalanx in the centre withdrew slowly in the face of the enemy. Though this could have come about as a result of the enemy phalanx's superiority, if true, it could also be a hint of the use of the feigned withdrawal to create confusion in the enemy ranks. As discussed above, the feigned withdrawal became a favoured tactic of Seleucid armies as it was in the battles of Philip II and Alexander. Antiochus III used it early in his reign outside the city of Atabyrium and gained a decisive victory. He tempted the garrison out to fight and pretended to withdraw down the hill, only to draw the enemy into an ambush and turn to encircle them (Polybius 5.70).

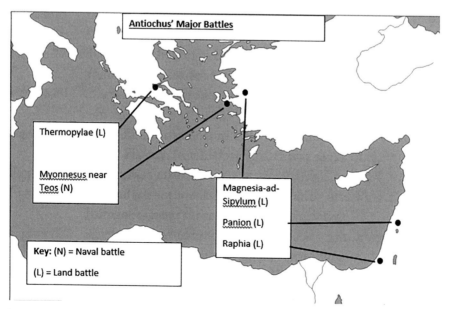

Figure 2. Map of Antiochus' major battles.

Summary

Thus, in conclusion, the Seleucid army of Antiochus III was very much like that of all other Hellenistic monarchs of the Macedonian style. It was a multi-ethnic and multi-faceted army reliant on a sarissa phalanx, a strong heavy cavalry unit and supporting light infantry and elephants, and at Magnesia there were chariots and camels. The tactics used were also variations on a theme: the hammer and anvil set-up and attack with protected flanks and the judicial use of a feigned withdrawal. The one main tactical departure was the lack of use of a withdrawn left flank. As we shall see, this ignored tactic, alongside his failure to fully integrate his battle plans and his pursuing the enemy too far, lost Antiochus numerous battles and eventually the western part of his empire to Rome.

Chapter Two

The Battle of Raphia

Antiochus III came to the throne at the age of 18 after the assassination of his brother Seleucus III as he embarked on a campaign against Pergamum. He had no military experience and relied almost exclusively on the advice of his council of generals and politicians.[1] This caused great friction, even at the beginning of his reign when two rival advisors developed factions offering conflicting advice. Antiochus only escaped from this when one advisor engineered the execution of the other; the second he eventually removed through another scheme.

Immediately Antiochus faced a rebellion of two brothers, Molon and Alexander, who were satraps in Mesopotamia of Media and Persis respectively (Polybius 5.43–46). He also needed to punish Egypt for the prior invasion that had humbled his father Seleucus II and to reconquer Syria. Moreover, under the reigns of his father Seleucus II and his brother Seleucus III, two major powers had developed unchecked in what had been Seleucid-controlled territory further east. The Bactrian kingdom, governed by the Greco-Macedonian satrap Diodotus and the original Western settlers, had declared independence from the Seleucids in the 240s under Seleucus II. Diodotus took advantage of Seleucus' civil war with his brother Antiochus Hierax and his Western focus. At the same time Arsaces, the new king of the Parni tribe of nomads from the Eurasian steppes, had successfully invaded and conquered the Seleucid satrapy of Parthia and shortly afterwards also conquered Hyrcania.

Seleucus II did retaliate to subdue the new threats within his borders, but after initially forcing Arsaces out of Parthia, he was defeated and perhaps captured during the Arsacid counterattack. By turning his focus west again to Egypt and Syria, Seleucus II ceded all control of the further east to these two new kingdoms. Seleucus' death closely followed by the assassination of his successor Seleucus III all but confirmed the establishment and longevity of both Parthia and Bactria as independent kingdoms.[2] Parthia famously went on to overcome and outlast both the Seleucids and Bactria in the East, becoming the Roman Empire's only rival for domination in the East for almost 300 years.[3]

Defeating the Rebels

As we can see, Antiochus III had a number of campaigns on his to-do list when he came to the throne. He, like most of his predecessors and successors, decided that going west to wrest control of Syria from Ptolemaic Egypt was the most important. Consequently, Antiochus trusted a general to deal with the brothers' rebellion in the east and tabled a counterattack against Parthia and Bactria until much later. Unfortunately, his general Xenoetas lost his life and most of his army in ignominious defeat when surprised by Molon and his brother as they counterattacked the camp he had just captured. Xenoetas had let his men enjoy the alcoholic spoils of victory in the abandoned enemy camp and Molon's unexpected return literally caught them with their pants down. Molon subsequently overran most of Mesopotamia including Babylon and the Eastern Seleucid capital Seleucia (Polybius 5.46–48).

Molon's great gains spurred Antiochus into action. He personally led the royal army eastwards and at the same time showed himself as the new king visiting his empire. His advance east over the two rivers into Apollonia threatened Molon's communication lines and drew him out to battle against Antiochus' superior army.

As discussed above, Antiochus fielded the standard Hellenistic army deployment of sarissa phalanx in the centre flanked by other heavy or medium allied or mercenary infantry. The heavy cavalry stood on both wings ready to assault the enemy and elephants, of which he had ten, and light infantry provided skirmishing along the flanks and possibly the centre. According to Polybius (Polybius, 5.53), Antiochus also posted reserves of light infantry and cavalry with the express purpose of surrounding the enemy. Though this tactic never happened because the rebel left wing switched sides, if true it suggests that Antiochus intended to use the horns of the buffalo tactic as described above. This would be the first time a Hellenistic general used that tactic. Hannibal of Carthage famously used the same tactic in his battles in Italy against the Romans to devastating effect. Had Antiochus surrounded the rebels, it would be the debut of this manoeuvre in a large-scale engagement in Mediterranean warfare predating Hannibal's more famous successes. Since he was fighting rebels, Antiochus or his advisors probably hoped that surrounding them would prompt them to surrender. As it was, that happened anyway without needing to surround them.

What is more interesting about this battle is the army deployment of Molon and the rebels. Polybius (5.53) describes the rebel army:

> However, he divided his cavalry between his two wings, taking into consideration the enemy's disposition, and between the two bodies of cavalry he placed the scutati, the Gauls, and in general all his heavy-armed troops. His archers, slingers and all such kind of troops he posted beyond the cavalry on either wing and his scythed chariots at intervals in front of his line.

In this conflict Molon commanded the more varied combined arms army. Though not stated, it is likely that he did field a sarissa phalanx in the centre. This was the standard for all armies of Macedonian heritage for more than 100 years, and the rebel strongholds of Media and Persis were important satrapies fortified by large numbers of Greco-Macedonian military settlers whose service in the phalanx was expected. That Molon also fielded Gauls despite commanding an army recruited away from Asia Minor where they had settled suggests perhaps that Gauls had spread throughout the Seleucid Empire as mercenaries at least. The scutati probably refers to soldiers armed with spear and shield, just as Macedonian hypaspists or Greek hoplites. Polybius earlier states that Molon wanted to fight in mountainous terrain to take advantage of his slingers, so these must have been some of his best troops. The deployment of all the light infantry on the wings suggests perhaps that Molon intended the missiles of these troops to keep the enemy cavalry at bay and prevent an outflanking manoeuvre of the exact kind that Antiochus planned. The scythed chariots were standard units of Media and Persis and therefore likely had to be in his army to appease the local aristocracy of the region. Their efficacy in battle was very little, as we shall see at Magnesia. Molon's cavalry, as usual, he expected to counter the charge of Antiochus' heavy horsemen.

For analytical purposes, it would have been most helpful had the rebels managed to fight a full battle against Antiochus to see how each side's tactics played out. As it is, we can only draw conclusions based on the deployment of the army and only then if we believe our one reliable source of Polybius. Nonetheless, it is clear that both sides relied on the standard deployment of the Macedonian-style army, but when in command of his unified empire Antiochus could call on a wide variety of units as he did at Magnesia.

After his victory over the rebels and finalizing the pacification of the central and northern satrapies, with a punitive invasion of those regions north of Media, Antiochus prepared to invade Syria. Antiochus launched his attack in the spring of 219. Though he gained the troops of Molon, the army he took into Syria was perhaps smaller than the one with which he faced down the rebels. It certainly was no more varied in terms of combined arms and he did not bring chariots with him.

Ptolemaic Army Training

Before we get to Antiochus' army it is important for comparison to review the army that the Egyptians prepared to defend Syria. Polybius (5.63) gives great detail about not only its composition but, for once, also its training. He states that they relied on Greek mercenary officers who had gained experience under the Macedonian kings and that 'They were most well advised in availing themselves of the services of these men, who having served under Demetrius and Antigonus had some notion of the reality of war of campaigning in general. Taking the troops in hand they got them into shape by correct military methods.'

What is most interesting is Polybius' description of what those correct military methods were. He states (5.64):

First of all they divided them according to their ages and nationalities, and provided them in each case with suitable arms and accoutrements, paying no attention to the manner in which they had previously been armed; in the next place they organized them as the necessities of the present situation required, breaking up the old regiments and abolishing the existing paymasters' lists, and having effected this, they drilled them, accustoming them not only to the word of command, but to the correct manipulation of their weapons. They also held frequent reviews and addressed the men, great services in this respect being rendered by Andromachus of Aspendus and Polycrates of Argos, who had recently arrived from Greece and in whom the spirit of Hellenic martial ardour and fertility of resource was still fresh, while at the same time they were distinguished by their origin and by their wealth, and Polycrates more especially by the antiquity of his family and the reputation as an athlete of his father Mnesiades. These with officers, by addressing the men both in public and in private, inspired them with enthusiasm and eagerness for the coming battle.

By breaking down the previous regimental organization the mercenary Greek officers were creating a new phalanx and army that was loyal to them and to Ptolemy. More importantly, they divided the army into logical new units that trained and served together, thus building a better unit cohesion and camaraderie among the soldiers that would serve them well in battle. By instituting very rigorous and extensive training in commands and weapon use they quickly transformed the army from one of raw recruits into one of reasonable discipline and confidence, though admittedly not battle-hardened or even tested. The battle reviews tested them and their learning and gave them practice in the manoeuvres they would need in battle. All these methods are the equivalent of basic training in modern armies. They took raw recruits and built a cohesive and confident fighting force from scratch through endless drill and exercises.

For anyone who is reading this and has never served in the military, perhaps the best way to appreciate the importance of this for a successful army is watching the epic TV drama series *Band of Brothers*. The first few episodes detail very well how to go about creating confidence in a new regiment of recruits for an imminent deployment to a daunting war that was already under way. The bonds built in this way through training and then shared experiences create friendships that last a lifetime. Also dependability on and confidence in the soldiers standing next to you on all sides creates a better fighting unit. Such bonds and confidence are absent in units of recruits that are press-ganged and conscripted into service and sent straight away to fight.

It is inconceivable that a modern army does not implement all these things in training, yet in the ancient world it was very rare. Conscription for immediate deployment was the usual methodology in ancient armies.

Rarely did commanders dedicate the time required to build the reliability of their army. This was especially true for such ethnically diverse forces as those that served in most Hellenistic armies, but especially that of Antiochus.

In fact, throughout the ancient world, our sources highlight for special praise the commanders who did drill and improve their soldiers. The most notable of all ancient Greco-Roman generals is the Athenian mercenary commander Iphicrates. Polyaenus' *Stratagems* is a work that simply lists the cunning strategies or tactics used by commanders in warfare up to the second century CE. It is organized by commander. Of all of the great commanders featured in the 900 entries such as Julius Caesar, Hannibal or Alexander the Great, Iphicrates receives the most air time. Iphicrates has sixty-three stratagems, while Caesar and Agesilaus are the next highest with thirty-three. Iphicrates' most famous contribution was to train his men to the highest standards and thus begin the era of the mercenary army. Alongside Iphicrates, generals such as Chabrias, Brasidas, Philip II and Antiochus III's contemporary Philopoemen receive special praise in various histories for knowing the importance of training their armies as well as they could.

The fulsome praise these men received from ancient commentators shows just how unusual it was to train an army extensively before embarking on a battle or campaign. It is true that every adult male in the ancient world had to serve in the army, so all men received exposure to battle from their early teens as soon as they were of a size to fight in the ranks. Those that survived gained valuable experience, but personal experience gained through random battles serving in random and different armies differs greatly from experience taught through countless hours of drill and training and the building of unit cohesion. The training is a necessary foundation on which to build the essential experience.

Therefore, although Antiochus' army had much greater levels of recent experience in battle, Ptolemy's was much better trained as a whole. As we shall see, this difference in training played a big part in the outcome of the battle. Yet even to Ptolemy's experienced officers, the army was untested and therefore still inferior to Antiochus. Nowhere was this truer than the important fighting in the sarissa phalanx. In that unit training and drills were paramount, but the experience of units led by battle-hardened veterans in the front few ranks generally made the difference in the melee. The famous unit of Silver Shields, veterans of Alexander the Great's campaigns and aged over 60, never lost an engagement even against well-trained phalanxes of much younger men. Such was their prowess that Antigonus Monophthalmus settled them as garrisons in a remote satrapy lest their arrogance in their own ability overcame their pliability as subordinate soldiers.

After the training of Ptolemy's army Polybius emphasizes that various officers received commands suited to their strengths and experience (Polybius, 5.65): 'All the men I have mentioned held commands suited to their particular attainments.'[4] It is clear that each officer was responsible for the drill of his own unit. In addition, it seems that each type of unit trained independently from the others in the army. This is a crucial part of combined arms as it allowed each unit to appreciate its own strengths and weaknesses and how it fitted into the whole army. It is also how modern armies prepare their disparate forces.

Polybius states that 'Eurylochus of Magnesia commanded a body of about three thousand men known as the Royal Guard, Socrates the Boeotian had under him two thousand peltasts', clearly distinguishing the elite infantry regiments from the rest. In this context, as others have argued, the term peltast refers to elite Macedonian heavy infantry.[5] These are the equivalent of the hypaspists of Alexander the Great, who were the elite regiment with soldiers selected on merit from every phalanx regiment. Hypaspists receive their name from carrying a large hoplite-sized shield, an aspis, so their name is 'hyp-' meaning 'under' and '-aspist' meaning 'shield-bearer'. The peltast, in this case, receives their name from carrying the distinctive pelte shield, a smaller northern Greek version of the aspis. Clearly, by the Hellenistic period the smaller and lighter pelte had replaced the aspis as the go-to shield for the mobile elite heavy infantry unit. Alexander had a unit of hypaspists as well as a royal guard regiment of Royal hypaspists. Though larger in number than Alexander's units, this is also likely the distinction in the Ptolemaic army here.

Polybius continues:

Phoxidas the Achaean, Ptolemy the son of Thraseas, and Andromachus of Aspendus exercised together in one body the phalanx and the Greek mercenaries, the phalanx twenty-five thousand strong being under the command of Andromachus and

Ptolemy and the mercenaries, numbering eight thousand, under that of Phoxidas.

Though they clearly maintained organizational separation between the Greek mercenaries and the phalanx, that both units trained together demonstrates that they fought next to each other in the line. This, as discussed above, was normal to protect the weaker flanks of the sarissa phalanx, especially one comprising new recruits, with the more defensive nature of experienced Greek hoplites and mercenaries.

For the cavalry the Egyptians continued the training regimen:

Polycrates undertook the training of the cavalry of the guard, about seven hundred strong, and the Libyan and native Egyptian horse; all of whom, numbering about three thousand, were under his command. It was Echecrates the Thessalian who trained most admirably the cavalry from Greece and all the mercenary cavalry, and thus rendered most signal service in the battle itself.

It is interesting to note that even among an army-wide training routine, Polybius is still able to draw attention to Echecrates as the one officer who completed the best training of his unit. Moreover, according to Polybius this extra special training allowed his unit to achieve the 'most signal service in the battle itself' as we will see shortly. Clearly Polybius is emphasizing the importance of training, something that is more understandable considering that Polybius wrote a specific work on tactics and training in a Hellenistic-style army. He also came originally from Achaea, the state whose army became the best in the Mediterranean because of the training regime implemented by its most successful general Philopoemen.

The training continued into the missile troops: 'and Cnopias of Allaria too was second to none in the attention he paid to the force under him composed of three thousand Cretans, one thousand being Neocretans whom he placed under the command of Philo of Cnossus.' These Cretans were archers, since that mode of fighting became synonymous with that region. Neo-Cretans likely came from the lower classes of Cretan society who were newly enfranchised and thus eligible to become archers in the Cretan allied contingent yet were still brigaded in a separate unit.

What is interesting in view of the unity of training given to the phalanx and Greek mercenaries is that sarissa armed Libyans received a separate designation, as do the Egyptian phalangites. 'They also armed in the Macedonian fashion three thousand Libyans under the command of Ammonius of Barce. The total native Egyptian force consisted of about twenty thousand heavy-armed men, and was commanded by Sosibius', showing that though it was a large phalanx, the officers did not trust it as much as the native Macedonian phalanx. That shows in its deployment and use in the actual battle as we shall see.

Polybius' description suggests that there were two distinct phalanx groups in the army. One was the reliable force of Macedonian and Greek settlers and the other, greatly inferior, was the unit of locally-raised and newly-trained Egyptians and Libyans. The sons of Greco-Macedonian settlers had the advantage of family tradition of serving in the phalanx and likely stories and tips they received from their fathers. That is probably what separated them from the Egyptians who, after all, trained the same amount, presumably, as the Macedonian and Greek troops. It is likely that the Greco-Macedonian phalanx troops were the established and experienced core of the Egyptian army and that these troops used this extra training to imbed into the unit cohesion any newer recruits alongside the veterans of prior campaigns. The Egyptian and Libyan phalanx was newly-created for this campaign and so did not have any actual battle experience to draw upon. No matter if the North African locals were better-trained than the Greco-Macedonians; it was experience of actual fighting in battle that schooled the phalanx, not the training ground. Of all the Hellenistic battles, Raphia is the one that makes that most clear.

Finally, to complete the light infantry, Polybius describes the usual force of Thracians and Gauls who would usually fight as javelin men:

and they had also collected a force of Thracians and Gauls, about four thousand of them from among settlers in Egypt and their descendants, and two thousand lately raised elsewhere. These were commanded by Dionysius the Thracian. Such were the numbers and nature of the army that Ptolemy was preparing.

In conclusion then, Ptolemy commanded a diverse but well-trained army with a large number of phalanx infantry and a well-martialled combined arms force, but many of the soldiers and units in the army had never fought in a proper battle. Until they did so, the Ptolemaic commanders remained unsure of how well they would fight against the experienced army of Antiochus.

When it came to the battle, Polybius (5.79) states that Ptolemy commanded an army of 70,000 infantry, 5,000 cavalry and 73 elephants. This is clearly an estimation of round figures as the more specific training totals given above total 65,000 infantry and 3,700 cavalry. It is likely that Polybius erred in the totals of some units in his training description. Echecrates the Thessalian commanded the mercenary cavalry, but no total for this unit appears. This one unit likely takes the cavalry total to 5,000. The missing 5,000 infantry probably comes from an approximation of each of the varied infantry units. Whatever the reason for the disparity, we can assume infantry of between 65,000 and 70,000.

Antiochus' Army

Antiochus' army then receives a detailed description from Polybius: 'Antiochus, on learning of his advance, concentrated his forces.' It is not clear if Polybius implies that this is the order of march or the order of the battle line, but he curiously separates the light infantry either side of the phalanx yet describes the cavalry all together. Taking the description in the order of Polybius summarized by type:[6]

Light infantry:
These consisted first of Daae, Carmanians and Cilicians, light-armed troops about 5,000 in number organized and commanded by Byttacus the Macedonian.

Heavy infantry of the phalanx:
Under Theodotus the Aetolian, who had played the traitor to Ptolemy, was a force of 10,000 selected from every part of the kingdom and armed in the Macedonian manner, most of them with silver shields. The phalanx was about 20,000 strong and was under the command of Nicarchus and Theodotus surnamed Hemiolius.

Missile infantry:
There were Agrianian and Persian bowmen and slingers to the number of 2,000, and with them 2,000 Thracians, all under the command of Menedemus of Alabanda.

<u>Light infantry:</u>
Aspasianus the Mede had under him a force of about 5,000 Medes, Cissians, Cadusians and Carmanians.
The Arabs and neighbouring tribes numbered about 10,000 and were commanded by Zabdibelus.
Probably heavy infantry hoplites:
Hippolochus the Thessalian commanded the mercenaries from Greece, 5,000 in number.

<u>Missile infantry:</u>
Antiochus had also 1,500 Cretans under Eurylochus and 1,000 Neocretans under Zelys of Gortyna.
With these were 500 Lydian javelineers and 1,000 Cardaces under Lysimachus the Gaul.
Cavalry, presumably light and heavy together:
The cavalry numbered 6,000 in all, 4,000 of them being commanded by Antipater the king's nephew and the rest by Themison.

<u>Total:</u>
The whole army of Antiochus consisted of 62,000 foot, 6,000 horse and 102 elephants.

Let us examine Antiochus' forces briefly. What is most notable is the number of distinct origins given for different units. Far more than the Ptolemaic army, Antiochus' forces came from all over his empire. This undoubtedly brought difficulties of communication and cultural differences. Most senior officers of each ethnic unit likely spoke Greek as the *lingua franca* of the period. Therefore, meetings of the general staff and even of the regimental commanders did not necessarily require translators, but the army had to camp separately and the individual soldiers likely had more differences from other units than shared similarities. Unlike the army of Alexander the Great that ended up being similarly diverse, all these soldiers had not suffered through the same hardships on campaign together and built that bond that comes from that. As a result, Antiochus and his advisors had to tread carefully in dealing with many different levels of experience, understanding and application in battle and on the march.

Though he could station similarly-armed troops together in the battle line, Antiochus could not necessarily guarantee that all troops of the same type would actually fight a battle in the same exact way. Perhaps different units of archers or slingers had different weapons that changed their range of fire, or perhaps some units of javelin men were comfortable in fighting at close quarters while others were not.

This could lead to problems when trying to implement a cohesive combined arms battle plan. Combined arms and integrated warfare getting the most out of every unit relies on an in-depth knowledge of the strengths and weaknesses of each specific unit. It is likely that Antiochus did not fully understand every unit since his army was too disparate and newly-collected. Moreover, the commander has to be confident that each unit will act correctly as told for any combined arms plan to work. At best it is likely that Antiochus could tell his officers what to do and simply hope that every unit would follow their orders. The army, though experienced in its core after his campaign against Molon, did not share enough collective experience of fighting the exact same battle tactics.

All the generals and officers of Alexander the Great and his Successors fought the battles in the same way. This built an innate confidence in the officers and the soldiers that they knew their role inside and out. Seleucid armies over the decades utilized varied battle plans and so the soldiers in the army could not exude the same confidence in carrying out their orders.

Antiochus himself was a veteran of only one battle as general. That prior engagement with Molon turned out to be an easy victory where the enemy units switched sides. So though man-for-man Antiochus' army had more experience than Ptolemy's, it was not such a difference as to convey superiority on Antiochus' army, especially considering that Ptolemy's officers were all extremely experienced.

The Battle Lines are Drawn

Ptolemy marched out for battle first. Both kings drew up their army in the now familiar traditional Macedonian deployment (Polybius, 5.82). Let us take each army in turn, unit by unit.

Ptolemy placed cavalry under Polycrates on the left. Then towards the centre came the Cretan archers and the elite regiments of the Royal Guard and the peltasts. Next to them was the unit of Libyan sarissa phalangites. This unit formed the left of the whole sarissa phalanx in the centre of the line. The Macedonian phalanx came, as usual, in the very centre. On their right came the Egyptian sarissa phalangites, on whose flank stood the Greek hoplite mercenaries of Phoxidas. Next to their right came the Thracian and Gallic javelin men and light infantry and on the extreme right wing was the mercenary cavalry of Echecrates. Forty elephants fronted the cavalry on the left wing and thirty-three on the right. Ptolemy fought with the elite heavy cavalry on the left.

This exactly matches the standard deployment of phalanx protected by hoplite heavy infantry on its flanks. Light and missile infantry then connect the heavy infantry to the cavalry on the wings. The elephants act as flank guards cementing the line in place while the faster cavalry charge the enemy. The one noticeable difference in Ptolemy's deployment is that the strike force of heavy cavalry was on the left wing, not the right, but this was undoubtedly to directly oppose Antiochus' own heavy cavalry. There is also again no indication that the line was drawn back at an angle.

Antiochus drew up his army similarly. He placed his strike force of 2,000 heavy cavalry on his right wing where he fought, and next to them another 2,000 cavalry stationed at an angle. Next came his Cretan (and Neo-Cretan) archers and then Greek mercenary hoplites next to a unit of Greek sarissa phalangites. The Macedonian phalanx took the centre. The Arian light infantry stood on their left flank and next to them the light infantry Medes, Cissians and Carmanians. Next to them came the Cardaces and Lydian javelin men missile infantry. Finally, more heavy cavalry held the

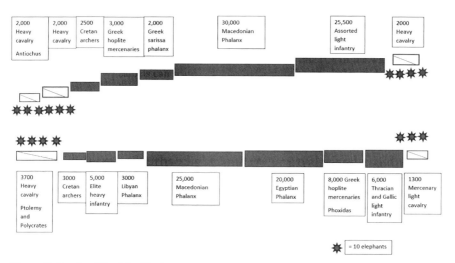

Figure 3. Battle of Raphia: Deployments.

extreme left wing. Sixty elephants stood in front of the right-wing cavalry and the remaining forty-two in front of the left-wing cavalry.

So, as usual, the two armies drew up opposite each other in exactly the same fashion. The one minor difference is that Antiochus did station a unit of cavalry on his right flank at an angle. This is an interesting departure since at first it seems like he is practising the preferred tactic of a withdrawn flank. However, he placed this unit of cavalry on his right flank from where he intended to personally lead his strike attack of heavy cavalry. Antiochus' 2,000 cavalry would charge the enemy line and the elephants would hold back to preserve the flank protection of the infantry. So not refusing the whole wing, the purpose of this cavalry is not clear. Perhaps it was to act as a reserve, or to shield the flank of Antiochus' own cavalry in expectation of Ptolemy's own cavalry attack. Whatever the reason, neither side utilized a refused flank and both kings intended to win the battle with a cavalry charge on the same wing in a direct duel of the princes.

This method had worked in past battles, most notably Eumenes' victory at the Hellespont over Craterus and Neoptolemus when Eumenes personally killed Neoptolemus (Diodorus, 18.29-32; Plutarch, *Eumenes* 7). However, it had also failed spectacularly, most notably with Eumenes' defeat at Gabiene against Antigonus Monophthalmus. So it was a risky tactic that could backfire spectacularly. Yet it was a sensible tactic of Antiochus since he enjoyed superiority in his heavy cavalry. It made sense for him to rely on that unit for his overall victory. Perhaps he enjoyed the chance to go toe-to-toe directly against his rival king and prove himself the better warrior. As we may expect, the outcome of the battle very much hinged on the success and effectiveness of Antiochus' cavalry attack but not for the obvious reason.

The Battle Rages

Both commanders personally began the attack opposite each other by sending their elephants forward. Polybius emphasizes that few of Ptolemy's elephants advanced because they were scared of the larger Indian elephants of Antiochus. Those that did fought well, apparently, animal to animal with each elephant also wearing a tower filled with missile troops.

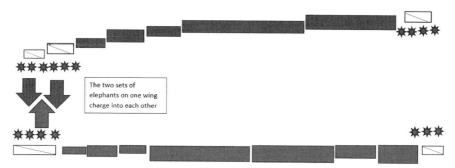

Figure 4. Battle of Raphia: Phase One.

Ptolemy's elephants fell back in disorder and disrupted the Egyptian cavalry behind them. Antiochus rode around the flank of the elephants and attacked the Ptolemaic heavy cavalry. At the same time Antiochus' Greek mercenary hoplites attacked the Egyptian heavy infantry peltasts and forced them back since the elephants had already disrupted their formation.

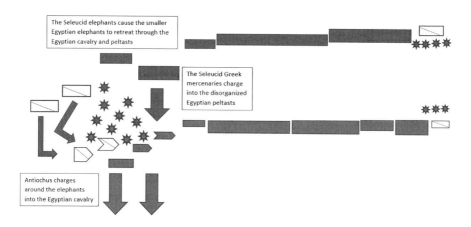

Figure 5. Battle of Raphia: Phase Two.

On the other wing Polybius clearly states that the Egyptian right-wing commander Echechrates was waiting to attack until the left-wing fight had resolved. This one small piece of information actually suggests that Ptolemy did hold back one wing in the standard refused flank tactic. On this occasion, it did not work since his attack force on the other wing failed spectacularly.

Echechrates noticed the dust rising from the other wing and correctly surmised that the Egyptian elephants and cavalry had routed. He then took the initiative and launched a counterattack while first moving the cavalry safely out from behind the Egyptian flank guard of elephants. He clearly expected a similar outcome in any elephant confrontation resulting in the chaos of crazed beasts. However, perhaps more importantly, in order to charge with his cavalry Echechrates had to ride around the elephants anyway just as Antiochus had done on the other wing. There was no way he could charge through them.

As discussed above, Polybius singled out Echechrates as the officer who had trained his men the best of the entire Egyptian army, and this training showed in the ease and success with which he was able to redeploy his men around the elephants. That Antiochus' left-wing cavalry did not attack perhaps also suggests that they too had orders to maintain a withdrawn flank and buy time for Antiochus to win on the right. If that is the case, they did not maintain a sufficient defensive posture and Echechrates' attack from the flank and rear completely overwhelmed them. At the same time that Echecrates attacked, the Ptolemaic Greek mercenaries successfully charged the Arabs on Antiochus' side and put them to flight.

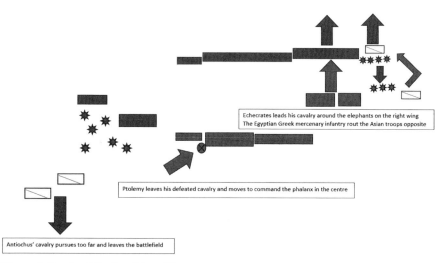

Figure 6. Battle of Raphia: Phase Three.

Thus the same story occurred on both sides. The Seleucid right flank had routed the Ptolemaic cavalry and the infantry that was to have shielded the phalanx's flank. The Ptolemaic right flank had done the same to the Seleucids. So the battle would be decided by the conflict of the phalanxes in the centre and who was best able to use the victorious cavalry on the flanks to attack the vulnerabilities of the phalanx in the centre.

Ptolemy had retreated from his defeated cavalry wing into the phalanx in the centre and his arrival prompted his men to fight more fiercely. It seems that Ptolemy's presence, added to the numerical superiority of the Egyptian phalanx gained the upper hand and forced the Seleucid phalanx to flee. In addition, although Polybius does not state it, Echechrates probably turned in on the exposed flank of the Seleucid phalanx in view of the expert training he had imparted onto his troops.

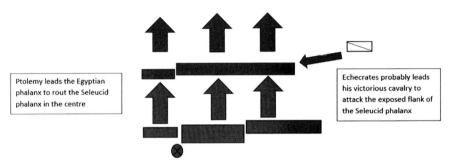

Ptolemy leads the Egyptian phalanx to rout the Seleucid phalanx in the centre

Echecrates probably leads his victorious cavalry to attack the exposed flank of the Seleucid phalanx

Figure 7. Battle of Raphia: Phase Four.

The determining factor in the battle revolved around Antiochus. Like many a cavalry commander before and after him, Antiochus in the elation of his victorious charge had pursued the enemy horsemen for a great distance. Polybius is clear that Antiochus gave no thought to the rest of the army or swinging his cavalry around to attack the centre of the Egyptian line. Rather he intently pursued the routing horses, completely oblivious to what was happening or would happen elsewhere. It took one of his officers to point out that the dust of the battle showed that the Seleucid phalanx had broken and was fleeing towards their camp. Antiochus reluctantly broke off his pursuit and, according to Polybius, believed that he lost the battle only because of the cowardice of his soldiers.

Polybius was right to blame his headlong charge on Antiochus' inexperience as a soldier and a general. It is a difficult thing to rein in elated horses and men and pull them away from plunder to another attack that may not be so successful and in which they may lose their own lives, but that is precisely the tactic that had to occur to win the battle. In every single one of his victories Alexander the Great only pursued the enemy cavalry once he was sure that the whole enemy army had fled. That is why it is such a point of emphasis when at the Battle of Gaugamela Parmenion sent a messenger to request Alexander to break off his pursuit to come to the aid of the beleaguered left wing (Arrian, *Anabasis*, 3.15). It was unusual for Alexander not to notice that himself.[7]

Though similarly inexperienced, Ptolemy had the foresight to show himself and encourage his men to victory even after Antiochus had outshone him in the cavalry engagement. Antiochus, however, charged off in a personal assault, seemingly not caring about the necessary role of the heavy cavalry as the hammer onto the anvil of the phalanx or the situation of the rest of his army. This lack of discipline in the charge and in implementing the overall battle plan cost Antiochus the victory and the war. Moreover, as we shall see, he had not learned his lesson by the time of the Battle of Magnesia.

Antiochus' flanking cavalry stationed at an angle never appear in Polybius' battle description. They perhaps remained behind the elephants to defend against any attack from Ptolemy's cavalry on the Seleucid flank. However, if this were the case, under the command of any decent officer they would have made use of the rout of the Egyptian wing and attacked the flank of the Ptolemaic phalanx. That they did not likely suggests that they joined in the pursuit of the routed Egyptian cavalry and also remained oblivious to their crucial battlefield role.

If Antiochus had ordered his left wing to avoid battle in order to buy time for the right to win, then that was the location to station a force of cavalry at an angle. Had this occurred, perhaps Echechrates' flank attack would not have been so devastating. However, Antiochus lost the battle not because Echechrates routed his left wing; rather he lost the battle himself by selfishly ignoring his duty to lead the cavalry to attack the exposed flank and rear of the Egyptian phalanx.

The Battle of Raphia should have resulted in a victory for Antiochus. He had arguably the better phalanx, better elephants, better cavalry, better elite and mercenary heavy infantry and more missile troops. He managed to snatch defeat from the jaws of victory by wasting all the successes enjoyed by these units against their Ptolemaic opponents. He made two crucial mistakes: his reckless personal charge, coupled with the lack of defensive organization on his left wing that exposed his weaker troops to Echechrates' charge. That Antiochus did not bring the cavalry back to attack the Ptolemaic centre exposed the veteran Seleucid phalanx to the larger and crucially entirely safe Ptolemaic phalanx so that eventually it retreated. The missile troops routed in the face of the Ptolemaic cavalry and the elephants remained isolated off to each side. Antiochus, entirely as a result of his own actions, denied his army an expected and perhaps empire-defining victory.

Antiochus, Prince Rupert and the Cavalry Charge of No Return

Antiochus is not the only cavalry commander to get carried away in the flush of a victorious charge and forget to help the rest of the army. Perhaps the most famous exponent of the invincible but tactically wasteful cavalry charge is Prince Rupert, the commander of the Royalist cavalry in the English Civil War.[8] In just his first engagement for the Royalist cause, a Parliamentary force arriving atop a hill out of a narrow lane caught Rupert by surprise since he had neglected to set sentries. Fortunately for Rupert, the enemy was as surprised as he and he was the first to act. He remounted his horse and personally charged straight into the enemy at the head, not even waiting a second for his men to join him. His furious attack instantly routed the enemy force and their entire troops fell back in chaos despite holding the advantage in numbers, training and discipline. This hugely successful cavalry charge was the hallmark of Rupert's career. Unfortunately, he never used it correctly in a full-scale battle.

At the first major battle of the Civil War at Edgehill, where Rupert's reputation went before him, the Royalist cavalry on both flanks of the Royal army easily routed their opposing numbers but pursued too far and began looting the enemy baggage train. It seems that Rupert had no care for returning to the fight. The Royalist infantry was also pushing back the enemy infantry in the centre, which had started to flee once they saw their cavalry routed. However, the Parliamentary army had two regiments of cavalry held in reserve and their arrival in the battle turned a definite rout into a virtual victory. King Charles I had no reserve cavalry to oppose the rampant enemy horsemen since they had all galloped off following Rupert. The Parliamentary cavalry was able to ride around imperiously routing various infantry regiments and even getting into the rear to attack the artillery and baggage. At the end of the day both sides had stemmed their various routing units and recalled the victorious ones to resume their original starting positions. It ended as a stalemate with neither side wanting to resume hostilities on the following day. However, every single commentator agrees, from 1640 until the present day, that had Rupert commanded the Royalist cavalry properly and turned to attack the enemy centre after routing the flanking cavalry, it would have been an overwhelming victory for the king and may have ended the entire war in one stroke. As it was, the war went on for four more years, famously witnessing the execution of King Charles I.

At the even more pivotal Battle of Naseby in 1645 Rupert's victorious cavalry on the right wing again rode off in pursuit and looting and failed to return, thus leaving exposed the right flank of their infantry. On the other wing the Parliamentary cavalry under Oliver Cromwell routed the Royalist cavalry and maintained a reserve to attack the Royalist infantry. Victory was assured once some defeated Parliamentary cavalry regiments from the left wing returned to join the fight and attack the exposed right flank of the Royalist centre. Rupert led countless cavalry charges in his numerous battles and routed the enemy force in most of them. However, he was rarely tactically astute enough to rally his troops to use their successful charge to bring about the overall victory of the army.

At Naseby the Parliamentarians would likely have won anyway regardless of Rupert's pursuit thanks to the brilliance of Oliver Cromwell as a cavalry officer of an opposite character to Rupert. Cromwell maintained a crucial discipline over his troopers and always saw the bigger tactical picture of the whole battle. Not once did he allow his entire cavalry to disappear in headlong pursuit but always sought the overall victory. Rupert too often got caught up in the moment and joined in the elation of chasing a fleeing enemy rather than corralling his men and returning to the fray. It is perhaps surprising that he did not return to battles since doing so would allow him to launch more cavalry charges on the enemy, which was clearly the thing he most enjoyed about soldiering. Whatever the reason, Rupert's inability to use a cavalry charge correctly cost him victories in his most important battles just as it did Antiochus; first here at Raphia and, more importantly, at Magnesia as we shall see.

Chapter Three

The Battles of Arius and Panion

After his defeat at Raphia Antiochus made a necessary peace with Ptolemy. He then turned north to deal with the regional Seleucid governor who had made himself independent. This Achaeus had helped place Antiochus on the throne after his brother's assassination, but had then decided to seek his own country as king of Asia Minor west of the Taurus Mountains. In a rapid campaign preceded by one of his generals, Antiochus bottled Achaeus up in his capital at Sardis (Polybius 10.28). Capturing the city by sending a small elite force to traverse a supposedly impassable ravine, Antiochus eventually took Achaeus prisoner. Some Cretans tricked Achaeus into thinking he would be rescued, only to capture him as soon as he was outside the citadel. According to Polybius, Cretans were proverbially synonymous with trickery just as they were with archery. After Achaeus' execution and the surrender of the citadel by his wife, Antiochus moved east to suppress a few rebel regions.

First he subdued Xerxes in Media Atropatene, modern-day Azerbaijan east of Armenia, by a show of force that prompted his submission. Antiochus restored his authority by marrying off his sister Antiochis in exchange for a tribute of money and horses. Then he marched into Parthia and Hyrcania to deal with the new Parthian threat of the Arsacid kings. Our sources are scanty for this expedition, but it seems that the Parthians fled into the mountains at Antiochus' onslaught after he arrived outside the capital Hecatompylos. Antiochus likely expected to fight a battle but it seems there was none and the Parthian forces melted away, probably over the mountains into their original steppes homeland. Antiochus crossed the mountains into Hyrcania, the neighbouring original satrapy also controlled by the Parthian kings. His tactics on getting through the fortified mountain passes are of note.

The Parthians had blocked the route through the pass expecting the phalanx and baggage animals but not expecting light troops to advance alone. Knowing that he had to find time and protection for his engineers to create a flat road for his phalanx and baggage, Antiochus sent ahead all his light infantry. Polybius (Polybius 10.29) even provides a marching order for these light troops, which separates them into distinct units according to the armaments. For our reconstruction of Antiochus' army this is most helpful and not usually provided by any sources. Light infantry usually appear in army descriptions all massed together indiscriminately. Polybius states that Antiochus divided these troops into three sections. The slingers, archers and mountain men accustomed to fighting well on rough terrain with javelins and stones went first. Then followed 2,000 Cretans with small shields, often called bucklers. At the rear came the rest of the light troops armed with breastplates and shields.

What we can see here is that Antiochus divided his forces according to tactical usage. He put the lighter ranged missile troops first to engage the enemy at a distance, but who had no efficacy in close or defensive combat. These would be true light infantry with next to no protective armour. Next came the Cretans with small defensive shields. These, then, were archers able to attack at range effectively but who also had some defensive armour for hand-to-hand conflict. Coming second, this substantial force could reinforce the lighter troops if they ran into difficulty. The final force wearing actual breastplates and shields fought like traditional Greek light peltasts, who could engage at a distance but hold their own in close combat if needed. Interestingly, Polybius does not mention the offensive armament for the Cretans or the third contingent. Clearly to him their defensive function outweighed their offensive in this context. The third group probably had javelins as well as swords for closer fighting. Just as I did above in describing an army according to military role not armament, so is Polybius doing here. Role in battle, especially in a combined arms system, was much more important than armament.

In the skirmishing the light troops traversed the rocky mountainside and caught the enemy outposts off guard since they expected attacks up the flatter terrain below. Polybius emphasizes that the stones coming from the slingers did the most damage. That is not surprising since an ancient expert slinger could fire stones or lead bullets more accurately, faster and further than ancient archers, hence the emphasis on slingers in the biblical story of David and Goliath. Polybius (10.30) states:

> In fact, by this means, with the slingers, archers and javelineers marching along the high ground in loose order, but closing up and occupying favourable positions, and with the Cretans covering their movements and marching parallel to them close to the defile slowly and in good order, the barbarians no longer stood their ground, but abandoning their positions collected on the actual summit of the pass.

Polybius states that the Cretans marched in good order lower down the slopes supporting the attacks of the lighter troops. It seems from Polybius' description that these Cretans did not need to engage the enemy much. Just their presence persuaded the Parthians to withdraw. Yet Cretans were first and foremost archers, and the sight of archers armed with small shields alone would not terrify outposts into retreating. It is more likely that they did fire arrows at the enemy, thus catching them in between missile fire from the bottom and top of the hilly slopes simultaneously. In good order probably refers to the discipline and organization of the Cretans in advancing in a well-drilled skirmishing line as archers. This was the forte of the Cretans by tradition and culture and so they certainly knew how to put on a show for the enemy.

These light troops forced out the enemy (Polybius 10.31) to allow for the engineers to clear the ground for the rest of the army. Once through the mountains, Antiochus captured numerous cities. The main one for which we have a description is his taking of Sirynx, the capital of the region. Well-defended with a triple moat and palisade, Antiochus used mines to bring down the walls and rocks to fill in the moats. Eventually his peltasts stormed the breach and he took the city.

These are not likely to be the armoured light infantry described above, similar to Greek peltasts. Rather it is the Macedonian term for peltasts as an elite heavy infantry regiment armed with spears, body armour and the pelte shield. The name for their shield being the same as that used by the lighter infantry of fourth-century Greece creates the confusion. This unit in Hellenistic armies always led assaults on breaches in city walls or across rivers into the faces of the enemy. Such an attack at close quarters can only succeed if carried out by experienced and well-trained heavy infantry. As discussed in the Introduction, these peltasts are equivalent to the hypaspists of Alexander the Great. This was his elite heavy infantry regiment that was mobile because of the linen armour they wore and their elite status, which also gained its name from its use of a shield, the aspis.

The Battle of the River Arius

After capturing these cities in the Parthian kingdom, Antiochus continued east to Bactria. Polybius suggests that this region was his primary goal since it offered more wealth and access to eastern trade than the Parthian-controlled territory. Moreover, the leading aristocrats and citizens of Bactria shared Antiochus' Greco-Macedonian heritage and so would be more likely to remain loyal in his empire. The new Bactrian king Euthydemus sent forward 10,000 Bactrian cavalry to oppose Antiochus' arrival and guard the crossing of the River Arius (Polybius 10.49). Bactrian cavalry were cataphracts, heavily armoured riders and horses, whose charge was like the later and more famous medieval knights.

Antiochus surprised the Bactrians by crossing the river before dawn with a small force of cavalry. The two sides fought a fierce cavalry engagement in which Antiochus apparently distinguished himself, losing a horse and receiving a wound to the mouth that took out some of his teeth. The Seleucid heavy cavalry held its own against the first regiment of the Bactrian cavalry, but fell back at the arrival of the second and third. However, organized Seleucid reinforcements attacked the Bactrians as they pursued Antiochus in disorder and forced them back in flight to the camp of Euthydemus.

It is not clear from Polybius exactly what type of Seleucid relief force pushed the Bactrians back. It was likely another force of cavalry, but could have been the light infantry as the advance guard of the whole army, or the actual army itself. Polybius implies that it was cavalry. Before the battle Antiochus 'called on one thousand of his cavalry who were accustomed to fight round him and ordered the rest to form up on the spot in squadrons and troops and all place themselves in their usual order', but he does not say who he left in command. Then Polybius states that Panaetolus advanced with his own men as the reinforcements. Not having a breakdown of unit commands in the whole army, it is difficult to tell which force this was. However, since it was a cavalry battle on a flat plain, that speed was important in saving Antiochus in time and that Antiochus had ordered the rest of the cavalry to form up in order behind him, the most likely force was the readied cavalry.

This battle does not provide any example of Antiochus' use of combined arms, but it does reiterate how successful a cavalry commander he was. Polybius singles him out for praise in leading the charge against the cataphracts, and if it was entirely a skirmish with cavalry then it was a great success against arguably the best cavalry force in the world. Again, this battle likens Antiochus to Prince Rupert as a cavalry commander among the best ever who could gain great victories in cavalry-only engagements. However, in more varied battles a lack of tactical awareness cost them dearly.

After the battle Euthydemus became afraid, according to Polybius, and retreated to his stronghold capital city of Bactra, modern-day Balkh in Afghanistan. Antiochus apparently besieged the city for two years or more without success. Unfortunately, no details survive concerning the siege or either army. A fragment of Polybius simply provides details of the peace treaty that ended the siege (Polybius 11.39). The siege was noteworthy among the Greeks and Romans afterwards because of the time involved. Polybius (29.12) includes it in a list of important sieges in a later section criticizing other historians for inventing details about them. We only know the time taken based on other events happening in Polybius' whole work and when Antiochus returned from the east.

Euthydemus argued that he had never rebelled against Antiochus but rather overthrown a dynasty of prior usurpers. He also rightly emphasized the importance of his position on the frontier in preventing warlike tribes from the steppes from crossing the mountains into the fertile plains of the Seleucid Empire. Antiochus agreed and allowed Euthydemus to keep using the title of King of Bactria in exchange for corn for his troops and enrolment into the Seleucid forces of all the Bactrian army's elephants. Antiochus cemented the treaty by betrothing his daughter to Euthydemus' son Demetrius (Polybius 11.34-39).

After pacifying Bactria, Antiochus continued across the Hindu Kush into India and met with the local king, Sophagasenus. Polybius again only summarizes what Antiochus received as the result of a final treaty before he left:

> Here he procured more elephants, so that his total force of them amounted now to a hundred and fifty, and after a further distribution of corn to his troops, set out himself with his army, leaving Androsthenes of Cyzicus to collect the treasure which the king had agreed to pay.

That he received elephants, corn and treasure without apparently ensuring a betrothal suggests that Antiochus may have defeated the Indians in battle. Either that or the Indian king paid to ensure that there was no need to fight one since the agreed price was even steeper than the one Euthydemus negotiated at Bactria. Moreover, the Indian kingdom was further away so that it was even less likely that a Seleucid king would return. It made sense for the Indian kingdom to stay on friendly terms with the Seleucids, if only to ensure the continued safety of their western border. However, to give up so much to ensure the continuation of that alliance was either extremely generous or necessary to avoid conflict or after a defeat.

In 180, twenty-five years after Antiochus' departure, Euthydemus' son Demetrius invaded and conquered much of north-western India. The Indo-Greek kingdom he established there became one of the strongest empires in the region and lasted for 200 years. The greatest king, Menander I, reconquered Bactria itself and expanded into parts of the Parthian kingdom, and later kings' dominion even extended to the borders of China. This suggests that the power of the Indian kingdoms was small and that Antiochus' show of force was enough to elicit such a fearful and generous payment to secure peace. However, we only have one side of Antiochus' agreement and it is possible that Antiochus did make some concessions to the Indian ruler.

The Battle of Panion

After his eastern sojourn ended, Antiochus returned west, fixing his eye again on Syria and war with Egypt. On his return to Seleucia, he received a generous gift from the city of Gerrha, a state on the western coast of the Persian Gulf, in return for peace and freedom of religion. Polybius states that he also sailed to the island of Tylus, near Bahrain, in the Persian Gulf. The submission of Gerrha must have been part of a larger campaign to establish Seleucid hegemony throughout the Persian Gulf (Polybius 13.9).

After this point only fragments survive of our principal source for Antiochus' reign, Polybius. Little is clear but in 205 or 204 Ptolemy IV died and his son and successor was only a boy (Polybius 15.20). Court politics led to a coup that resulted in a great changing of the guard of the principal ministers (Polybius 15.25-36). In the midst of this chaos it seems that the two great Hellenistic kings, Philip V of Macedon, now dominant in Greece, and Antiochus agreed to attack Egypt and carve up the kingdom.[1] Polybius mentions the pact repeatedly but never specifically as a *casus belli* for the Roman intervention in Greece, Egypt and Syria. Some historians doubt the existence of the pact at all.[2] However, we can perhaps assume it was a crucial aspect since Polybius' actual description of the pact does not survive but the section following its likely location is a long diatribe on the bad characters of Philip and Antiochus in making such a terrible agreement (Polybius 15.20). Regardless, Antiochus used the chaos in Egypt as a reason to launch another invasion of Syria. This time the somewhat confusing description of Polybius does provide a breakdown of each army and the tactics of the battle.

As discussed above, Polybius' description of the Battle of Panion (16.18–9) is mainly a critique of the description of another historian's account of the same battle. Despite this confusing narrative, we can piece together certain aspects of the armies and battle for certain and others that are likely.

The Egyptian army led by Scopas placed its phalanx in the centre of its line on level ground and cavalry on either side, with the right flank resting on some hills. However, Polybius suggests in his following description that Antiochus' right wing rested on the hill commanding the enemy. If this is the same hill, then it cannot be both armies' right wing. More likely, there were two hills on either side of the field and each army rested its right wing on one.

At night, Antiochus sent cavalry to occupy the hills overlooking the enemy under his son Antiochus and then crossed the river between the two camps to draw up his army on the plain opposite Scopas' forces. Again, as usual, he placed cavalry on either side of the phalanx. Polybius is clear that his right-wing cavalry featured a unit of cataphracts. This heavily-armoured cavalry unit discussed above fought in a Seleucid army for the first time at Panion. It must have joined Antiochus' army after his earlier subjugation of the Greco-Bactrian kingdom. His son Antiochus commanded the right wing.

The description of Zeno as narrated by Polybius (16.18-9) states:

Next he tells us that the king posted the elephants at some distance in advance of the phalanx together with Antipater's Tarantines, the spaces between the elephants being filled with bowmen and slingers, while he himself with his horse and foot guards took up a position behind the elephants.

Polybius takes this to mean that Zeno is completely wrong, since it makes no sense for elephants and cavalry to fight directly in front of the phalanx, but Zeno does not say that. Rather he suggests that Antiochus' left wing, which he seems to be describing here in its usual deployment, stood a little in front of the position of the phalanx; not directly in front, but off to the side though further forward in being nearer the enemy line. This is not unusual. In fact, it is the normal deployment if Antiochus planned to hold back the rest of his line or the enemy flank with this oblique formation. As discussed above, and in detail elsewhere, the oblique battle line was the standard tactical deployment of almost all Hellenistic battles in the fourth century and later.

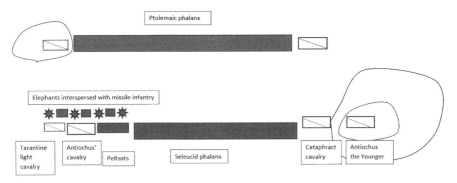

Figure 8. Battle of Panion: Deployment.

Polybius furthers his confusion in this regard when he criticizes Zeno's account of the battle. Polybius states: 'He tells us that the younger Antiochus, whom he stationed in command of the mailed cavalry on the plain opposite the enemy's left, charged from the hill, routed and pursued the cavalry under Ptolemy, son of Aeropus, who commanded the Aetolians in the plain and on the left.'

  This is exactly what happens in all Hellenistic and especially Seleucid battles. The Seleucid heavy cavalry force on the right wing, in this case commanded by Antiochus' son, easily routed the opposing cavalry.

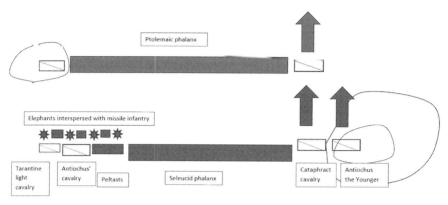

Figure 9. Battle of Panion: Phase One.

Zeno continues that, as you would expect, 'the two phalanxes met and fought stubbornly' in the centre of the line. Polybius continues criticizing Zeno for 'forgetting that it was impossible for them to meet as the elephants, cavalry and light-armed troops were stationed in front of them'. He criticizes the phalanx confrontation based solely on his misunderstanding of Zeno's statement of elephants deployed in front of the phalanx. In reality, the phalanxes could and certainly did meet in the centre since Antiochus' force of 'elephants, cavalry and light-armed troops were stationed in front of them' but off to their left protecting their flank. An understanding of the usual deployment of a Hellenistic army reveals that Polybius is wrong and Zeno is actually right.

In this we should censure Polybius and take him to task, just as he requests of future historians (16.20):

> And I too will beg both my contemporaries and future generations in pronouncing on my work, if they ever find me making misstatements or neglecting the truth intentionally to censure me relentlessly, but if I merely err owing to ignorance to pardon me, especially in view of the magnitude of the work and its comprehensive treatment of events.

Antiochus' deployment on the left flank actually mirrors his deployment at Raphia, with his personally-led horse guards immediately behind the flank guard of elephants. The difference this time is that he also had light cavalry, the Tarantines, presumably to shield the flank of the elephants, and missile infantry between the elephants. Such a deployment of missile infantry had become standard in Hellenistic armies of the late third century.

Polybius continues in his criticism of Zeno:

> Next he states that the phalanx, proving inferior in fighting power and pressed hard by the Aetolians, retreated slowly, but that the elephants were of great service in receiving them in their retreat and engaging the enemy. It is not easy to see how this could happen in the rear of the phalanx, or how if it did happen great service was rendered. For once the two phalanxes had met it was not possible for the elephants to distinguish friend from foe among those they encountered.

Polybius is again confused about how the elephants can do service for the phalanx in its retreat in the rear since he believes Zeno places the elephants in front of the phalanx. However, if the elephants actually stood on the left flank of the Seleucid phalanx, then as the phalanx gave ground the elephants could attack the exposed right flank of the advancing Egyptian phalanx. This would indeed cause significant chaos in the Egyptian ranks as the large beasts ploughed into the vulnerable flank of the phalanx. It also explains why the elephants did not confuse friend with foe and cause casualties in the Seleucid phalanx by mistake. The elephants would only attack the flanks of the Egyptian phalanx while the Seleucid one continued backing away, or more likely turned to press the attack from the front. Since the length of the sarissas of the two phalanxes would maintain a significant gap between the front ranks of each unit, distinguishing each unit would be easy, one facing one way and one the other.

Moreover, this positioning of the elephants on the left flank actually also helps explain Zeno's next details with which Polybius finds fault. He states:

> In addition to this he says the Aetolian cavalry were put out of action in the battle because they were unaccustomed to the sight of the elephants. But the cavalry posted on the right remained unbroken from the beginning as he says himself, while the rest of the cavalry,

which had been assigned to the left wing, had been vanquished and put to flight by Antiochus. What part of the cavalry, then, was it that was terrified by the elephants in the centre of the phalanx, and where was the king all this time and what service did he render in the action with the horse and foot he had about him, the finest in the army? We are not told a single word about this.

The Aetolian cavalry that fled was likely a force of cavalry assigned to shield the right flank of the advancing Aetolian phalanx in the Egyptian army. This cavalry force, seeing the Seleucid phalanx going backwards, probably expected to wheel around Antiochus' left-wing guard of elephants and attack the exposed flank of the Seleucid phalanx. However, before they could do that Antiochus' elephants charged. When the elephants charged into the Egyptian right wing, before they caused carnage in the Aetolian phalanx they caused the Aetolian cavalry to retreat. This unexpected retreat of the Aetolian cavalry exposed the Egyptian phalanx to a flanking attack from the elephants.

Scopas, the Egyptian general, likely intended the Aetolian cavalry to shield his phalanx and hopefully rout or at least turn the Seleucid cavalry opposite them. This did not happen because they were unaccustomed to the sight of the elephants. When Zeno states that the Egyptian right-wing cavalry had remained unbroken from the beginning, he perhaps means that they remained unbroken until this point when the Aetolian cavalry fled before the elephant charge or that the unit remained unbroken; it just fled together en masse but without breaking apart.

When Polybius criticizes Zeno for not stating what Antiochus' force of elite guard cavalry and infantry was doing, he perhaps does not grasp how total the Seleucid victory was on this flank. Antiochus, as in Raphia and as in other Hellenistic battles, waited with his troops until the elephant engagement raged before intending to lead his elite forces on an assault on the enemy flank around the side of the elephants. This exact manoeuvre had caused the Ptolemaic wing to disintegrate completely at Raphia and there is no reason why Antiochus would doubt that the same thing would occur again. However, in this case the elephant charge was so successful in breaking the Egyptian wing that he did not need to lead his men around them.

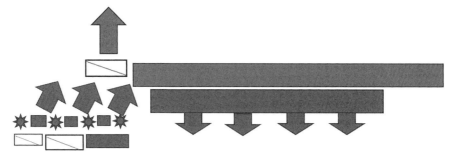

Figure 10. Battle of Panion: Phase Two.

The retreat of the Aetolian cavalry at the onset of the elephants won Antiochus the initiative in the battle on that flank already. He then enjoyed the luxury of keeping his best troops in reserve until the opportune moment. Why commit expensive elite veteran troops to battle if it is already going your way?

It is important to note here that the Egyptian army did not have elephants. At Raphia Antiochus had to attack with his cavalry around the elephant-on-elephant melee in front of him. At Panion there was no elephant melee and the Seleucid animals could charge directly against the enemy as a precursor to Antiochus' elite forces following up with another charge. Such a double charge would cause significant damage to soldiers and morale in the Egyptian ranks.

Polybius continues criticizing Zeno in his account of the conduct of the Egyptian general Scopas, but this actually helps explain what Antiochus' cavalry force did:

> And can he explain how Scopas was both the first and the last to leave the field? For he tells us that when he saw the younger Antiochus returning from the pursuit and threatening the phalanx from the rear he despaired of victory and retreated; but after this the hottest part of the battle began, upon the phalanx being surrounded by the elephants and cavalry, and now Scopas was the last to leave the field.

Again, we can make sense of Zeno's description of Scopas if we consider what Antiochus himself did with his best cavalry after the elephant charge was so successful. Though Antiochus did not need to support the elephants, which remained engaged with the Egyptian phalanx, he likely would not remain completely inactive. As Polybius states, it would be surprising if he did not make use of his best troops somehow. The easiest and most tactically astute manoeuvre to make was to ride around the elephants and attack in the rear the Egyptian phalanx now shorn of cavalry support. This is exactly what Zeno states occurred in the battle: 'After this the hottest part of the battle began, upon the phalanx being surrounded by the elephants and cavalry', when Scopas decided to retreat. The elephants are likely those from the Seleucid left wing that plunged into the phalanx, so the cavalry are likely the ones Antiochus commanded behind the elephants.

When Zeno states concerning Scopas that 'when he saw the younger Antiochus returning from the pursuit and threatening the phalanx from the rear he despaired of victory and retreated', he means that he gave the order for the whole army to retreat. It is common for historians to use the name of the general to refer to the whole army. Caesar is a famous master of that in his *Gallic Wars*. Surrounded already by elephants and cavalry from Antiochus' victorious left wing, as soon as he saw the younger Antiochus' cavalry reappearing on the battlefield behind him, Scopas ordered his army to retreat. Then we can add in the statement, 'Scopas was the last to leave the field.' He gave the command to retreat when he saw Antiochus the Younger's cavalry threatening his army's withdrawal to the camp and then retreated himself only once the rest of his army had successfully disengaged and made it out to safety.

Once he was sure the Aetolian cavalry had fled completely, perhaps chased by the Tarantine cavalry, Antiochus launched his elite forces into the rear of the Egyptian phalanx. Polybius unknowingly confirms this later when he states that the Egyptians fled 'the phalanx being surrounded by the elephants and cavalry', although he does not specify which cavalry. He believes that it was the cavalry from the right wing that returned to the battle after routing its opposite horsemen. Unless the Egyptians failed to watch their rear and did not see the return of the Seleucid cavalry, Scopas would try to extract what was left of his army before his rear and avenue of escape were completely cut off by that victorious force. To do any less would be military suicide. Once surrounded, there would be no way to win and no way to survive. That Scopas escaped with a large chunk of his army suggests that an avenue of retreat was available. The cavalry that according to Polybius surrounded the phalanx must be Antiochus III's cavalry, not that returning from the right wing led by Antiochus the Younger.

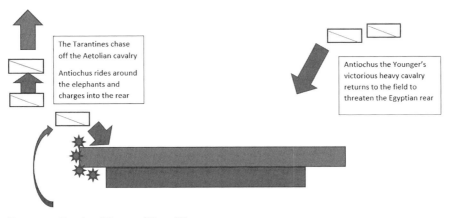

The Tarantines chase off the Aetolian cavalry

Antiochus rides around the elephants and charges into the rear

Antiochus the Younger's victorious heavy cavalry returns to the field to threaten the Egyptian rear

Figure 11. Battle of Panion: Phase Three.

Other historians, when attempting to reconstruct the events of this battle, take Polybius at his word for his criticisms of poor old Zeno. They too then try to explain like Polybius how the phalanxes of each side can fight against each other when the Seleucid cavalry, elite infantry, missile infantry, Tarantines and elephants fought in front of them. Usually the explanation is the creation of gaps in the Seleucid phalanx to allow the elephants, cavalry and light troops through before they engaged with the Egyptian phalanx, or as they retreated. Yet exactly as discussed by Polybius, such a manoeuvre would be foolhardy to say the least.

The strength of the phalanx was in presenting an unbroken line of sarissas to the enemy. Any gaps in the formation of the phalanx could prove fatal, as at so many other battles. Moreover, any gaps big enough to let through 100 elephants as well as accompanying soldiers and cavalry would be too large to close again before the enemy phalanx covered the distance between the lines. However, we have no statement that the Seleucid phalanx fled completely, which would have allowed elephants to come through their line. Zeno's description simply states that the elephants received the Seleucid phalanx and did great service. This must have taken place on its flank, not in its front. In the context of a Hellenistic battle, what greater service is there to a phalanx than performing a devastating flanking attack on the enemy phalanx just as it bears down? It would be very strange for elephants to arrive through the middle of gaps in the Seleucid phalanx in order to stop the Egyptian phalanx's advance only to then move around and attack the phalanx on its flank. Elephants do not move quickly at tight angles and if coming through the centre of the Seleucid line would have certainly simply charged straight ahead into the enemy phalanx. Such an assault would not have been as disastrous to the phalanx since the dense hedge of sarissas facing the elephants would disconcert the animals just as it did in preventing horses from charging a phalanx head-on.[3]

Therefore, despite Polybius' criticisms of Zeno's account, the only fact he actually got wrong was to place two different sons of Antiochus on the field both called Antiochus. According to Zeno, Antiochus III's elder son named Antiochus led the advance cavalry controlling the hills, while his younger son, also named Antiochus, commanded the right wing. Polybius correctly censures Zeno for this error since only Antiochus' elder son was at the battle. His younger son was only 15 at the time, perhaps too young to serve in the army and certainly too young to command the entire right wing in place of his older brother. Moreover, the younger son's name was initially Mithridates and he was only renamed Antiochus when he became king in 175.

Perhaps Zeno confused the hills in his description. As discussed above, Zeno states that Scopas placed his right wing on the hills and that Antiochus the Younger went at night to command the hills overlooking the field. If this is the same hill, then this Antiochus cannot have commanded the Seleucid right wing. Zeno perhaps then misunderstood and posited a second Antiochus, one to command the right wing and another holding the hill on the Egyptian right wing (Seleucid left). The fact that in history two of Antiochus III's sons were known by the name Antiochus would help to justify his assumption. Zeno was unaware that the younger son only received that as a regnal name of Antiochus IV decades later. It is easier, as I have done, to instead understand Zeno's description to refer to two sets of hills, one on the Egyptian right and one on the Seleucid right. Thus, there need only be one Antiochus the Younger as Polybius confirms.

Yet perhaps Polybius completely misunderstands Zeno. Just as I do above, when describing the actions of Antiochus III the king and of his son Antiochus, it is easier to utilize the phrase 'the younger Antiochus' with reference to the son. Perhaps when describing the initial occupation of the high ground by the cavalry Zeno referred to this son as Antiochus III's eldest son, also called Antiochus. This was likely the first time he appears in Zeno's account and so he was explaining to his audience who this new Antiochus was. Later, when Zeno describes the actions of the right-wing cavalry he states that the younger Antiochus commanded there. He does not mean the younger son of the king named Antiochus, but the younger Antiochus fighting at the battle. This seems to me to be a natural way of describing the son of Antiochus in the battle. Polybius probably believed that Zeno made an error in introducing the second younger son, when in reality the younger comparison adjective refers to the son being younger than his father.

Tactics at Panion

Having made sense of Zeno's description, we can actually go further into analyzing Antiochus' tactics at this battle. At first sight it seems strange for Antiochus to place his left wing so significantly far in front of the central phalanx if he is not holding back his other wing to match the oblique battle line. Yet it makes perfect sense if the retreat of the Seleucid phalanx in the centre was a planned move in order to draw the Egyptian forces forward and expose their flank. Antiochus used the slow retreat of the phalanx to draw the enemy out to where he wanted them, and he was able to launch his elephants at their flank seemingly unopposed by any Egyptian elephants.

This is a perfect use of the feigned withdrawal that was a standard part of the Seleucid phalanx's training as discussed above. It is also the only logical explanation for why Antiochus would advance his left wing so much. Moreover, if Antiochus' elephants did not face an opposing force of Egyptian animals then he would have been certain that nothing could prevent his elephants charging straight into the enemy phalanx's vulnerable flank. Though we only have Polybius' critique of Zeno's description as evidence for this battle, Egyptian elephants are noticeably absent from both. Moreover, if Zeno is right that the Aetolians fled because they were unfamiliar with the elephants, Antiochus must have guessed that this would happen. He likely knew from his scouts and deserters that Aetolians formed the core of the Egyptian army, and perhaps even knew on which wing Scopas stationed them. Guessing they would flee before an elephant charge, he stationed himself on the left to make sure everything on this wing went according to plan. Antiochus knew his elephants could charge unopposed into the enemy line and so he planned accordingly. He stationed them as the most advanced part of his line protected by strong cavalry forces and missile infantry. He ordered his phalanx to feign a withdrawal to draw out the enemy phalanx and cavalry and then launched a devastating and battle-winning charge into their flank.

This is the most likely scenario since Antiochus did not station elephants on his right wing too as he usually did. This battle is one of very few where generals did not divide elephants between the two wings of the army. To break from the usual formation is notable. With no Egyptian elephants in opposition, Antiochus had free rein to choose from where to attack with his. Moreover, for once he did not have to prepare for an elephant-on-elephant battle. Therefore, he could use elephants as a shock force to charge the enemy, something that enemy elephants prevented. His decision to place them on the left wing rather than the traditional assault location on the right was perhaps to give space on that wing for Antiochus the Younger and the cataphracts to charge down from the hill. He may also have known that the Aetolians stood on the Egyptian right wing and that they would not be familiar with elephants in battle. Alternatively, he perhaps wanted to use his elephants to shield the flank of his phalanx when expecting the main Egyptian assault force to attack his left wing as was traditional. Whatever the initial tactic that motivated the placement of the elephants, their unopposed presence proved the decisive factor in defeating the larger and better Egyptian phalanx.

In this light, it is important to note that Antiochus' son led his right-wing cavalry of heavy cataphracts in the usual assault. The king usually occupied this position of glory and led the decisive cavalry charge. It is how Antiochus fought at all his other battles: Raphia, Arius and Magnesia. Therefore, the one instance where Antiochus fought in a different location is likely of utmost significance. This is the one battle where Antiochus did not rely solely on a right-wing heavy cavalry charge for victory. He came up with a different and innovative strategy to win the battle on both wings instead. His son led the cavalry charge with the expected result of routing the enemy wing, but this time he took command on the other wing with the more complicated tactic of exploiting the Egyptian army's vulnerability to elephants.

It was a tradition in Seleucid armies for eldest sons to gain experience by commanding a cavalry squadron. Antiochus I had led the Seleucid cavalry at Ipsus while his father Seleucus commanded the reserve elephant line. Ipsus is a perfect comparison to Panion, since in both cases the eldest son commanded the heavy cavalry with an important mission while the king commanded an elephant force on whose actions rested the outcome of the battle. At Ipsus Seleucus, using elephants to block the return of Demetrius' victorious cavalry, won that battle for the allies. The role of the future Antiochus I in retreating and drawing Demetrius' force away was crucial in creating the space and time for Seleucus to deploy the elephants. At Panion, Antiochus led the elephants into a flanking attack of the Egyptian phalanx, the manoeuvre that decided the battle. However, Antiochus the Younger's cavalry charge had pushed all supporting Egyptian cavalry away, thus leaving the phalanx exposed to the attack of Antiochus' elephants and cavalry. The mere sight of his return to the battlefield was enough to cause Scopas to order the general retreat of the Egyptian army. Again, it seems, Antiochus was using tried and trusted Seleucid tactics in this battle to great effect.

Therefore, if we have reconstructed the battle correctly, Antiochus' greatest tactical triumph was at the Battle of Panion. Here he successfully used an advanced left flank, feigned withdrawal, elephant charge and a right- and left-wing heavy cavalry hammer onto an unbroken phalanx

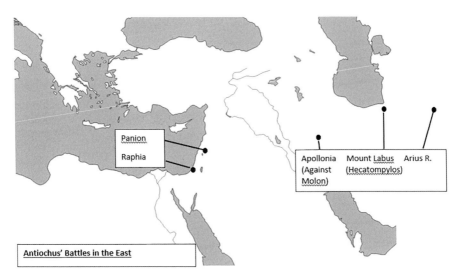

Figure 12. Map of Antiochus' battles in the East.

anvil in the centre. It is the only occasion where Antiochus, or any later Hellenistic general, utilized to perfection in one single engagement all the battle tactics introduced and perfected by Philip and Alexander the Great and the heavy elephant charge of Pyrrhus. It is his victory at Panion for which Antiochus should be lauded as a brilliant general, not his sojourn through the east, and it exonerates him somewhat for his spectacular and more politically important failures in generalship at Raphia and Magnesia.

Chapter Four

The Coming of Rome and the Battle of Thermopylae

After his huge success at Panion, Antiochus had Egypt where he wanted. Though no source describes in detail what happened next, one fragment of Polybius (16.39) states that he 'occupied Samaria, Abila and Gadara, and after a short time those Jews who inhabited the holy place called Jerusalem surrendered to him'. It seems that he then refrained from invading Egypt itself, which may not have been his goal anyway. He instead turned towards Ephesus, according to Polybius (18.40a) as a place he had long coveted.

Unfortunately, no source records in detail what Antiochus did between Panion in 200 and his invasion of Caria and Asia Minor in 197. From 197 Livy, rather than the fragmentary history of Polybius, now becomes the best source for tracing Antiochus' movements and the beginnings of his dispute with Rome. He states:

> During the previous summer Antiochus had reduced all the cities in Coelo-Syria which had been under Ptolemy's sway, and though he had now withdrawn into winter quarters he displayed as great activity as he had done during the summer. He had called up the whole strength of his kingdom and had amassed enormous forces, both military and naval. At the commencement of spring he had sent his two sons, Ardys and Mithridates, with an army to Sardis with instructions to wait for him there whilst he started by sea with a fleet of a hundred decked ships and two hundred smaller vessels, including swift pinnaces and Cyprian barques. His object was twofold: to attempt the reduction of the cities along the whole coastline of Cilicia, Lycia and Caria which owed allegiance to Ptolemy, and also to assist Philip – the war with him was not over – both by land and sea.

Once Antiochus had control of Coele-Syria, the goal of all these Seleucid-Ptolemaic wars, he moved to re-establish control over Asia Minor, possibly with the intention of eventually threatening Pergamum and Rhodes. Both these states were independent with growing areas of influence on the coast of Asia Minor and blocked Antiochus' route to the Hellespont if he wished to cross into Thrace and mirror the conquests of his ancestor Seleucus I.

As Livy states, Antiochus may also have intended to move towards Macedon to help Philip in his war against the Romans. He would have known of its course since the pact discussed above nominally bound the two kings, but he only sought to intervene when it was in his best interests. Philip certainly did not request direct aid from Antiochus before his disastrous defeat at Cynoscephalae in 197. The early phase of the Second Macedonian War suggested that Philip could hold his own against the Romans and even contemplate victory. Without a direct appeal, Antiochus spent his time securing his own new conquests over Ptolemaic Egypt. Once he secured those, he could move north to aid Philip at least by changing to him from Philip the focus of Pergamum and Rhodes, two key states allied to Rome. It is unlikely he actually intended to land an army to help Philip. To do so would be to abandon his own borders, and the pact of the kings likely did not include mutual direct military aid since it was offensive against Egypt, not mutually defensive.

Indeed his advances in Asia Minor did include the invasion of territory belonging to Attalus, the king of Pergamum. Livy records an embassy in Rome in 198 from Attalus requesting that they send troops to aid him in opposing Antiochus, or if they could not spare troops to allow him to take back the fleet and soldiers he lent to Rome. The Roman Senate replied that they could not attack Antiochus since they were on friendly terms, but they would send word for him to stop attacking another Roman ally in Pergamum. Their message ended (Livy 32.8): 'It is only just and right that monarchs who are allies and friends of Rome should also keep the peace towards each other.' This shows where Antiochus' focus was but also his current warm relationship with Rome. A later embassy from Attalus sending thanks to Rome confirms that Antiochus did withdraw from Pergamene territory at the arrival of Rome's ambassadors (Livy 32.27).

However, Antiochus continued to pressure the territory of Rhodes. Livy (33.20) records that the Rhodians sent Antiochus an ultimatum not to bring his fleet past a key promontory in Cilicia or they would have to attack him:

> Antiochus was at the time investing Coracesium. He had so far secured Zephyrium, Soli, Aphrodisias and Corycus, and after rounding Anemurium – another Cilician headland – had captured Selinus. All these towns and other fortified places on this coast had submitted to him either voluntarily or under the stress of fear, but Coracesium unexpectedly shut its gates against him.

Antiochus rebuffed the Rhodian threat, arguing that he was on friendly terms with Rome and did not threaten their interests. Rhodes did not attack him but instead used diplomacy and provided other assistance to save cities often simply by giving advanced warning of Antiochus' movement: 'It was thus that Caunos, Myndus, Halicarnassus and Samos owed their liberty to Rhodes.'

Whatever Antiochus' goals or his activities before the spring of 196, the victory over Philip at Cynoscephalae allowed the Romans to focus on Antiochus in order to ensure the independence of their increasingly threatened allies on the Eastern Mediterranean coast. Livy (33.27) records that after Cynoscephalae Flamininus wanted to pacify affairs in Greece quickly because he was suspicious of Antiochus' activities. Then later in 196, when ten Roman commissioners decided on the liberation of Greek cities from Roman garrisons, the Romans maintained control of three key sites specifically because they feared an invasion of Antiochus (Livy 33.31).

Rome Gets Involved

The key shift in Roman attitude towards Antiochus pressing too much in Asia Minor was clear when his ambassadors met the commissioners and professed the same friendship they had earlier. On this occasion, now free from the worries of the Second Macedonian War, the Romans made their position clear as the new defenders of the freedom and independence of Greek cities. It was very different and vehemently opposed to Antiochus (Livy 33.34):

Antiochus was openly and unequivocally warned to evacuate all the cities in Asia which had belonged to either Philip or Ptolemy, to leave the free States alone, and never to make aggressions on them, as all the cities through the length and breadth of Greece must continue to enjoy peace and liberty. He was especially warned not to lead his forces into Europe or go there himself.

With that ultimatum it was clear to Antiochus that he had to forego his ambition of expanding his empire into Asia Minor unless he wanted to face the might of Rome. Yet such was Antiochus' determination and belief after his decade or more of conquest and success that the threat did not deter him.

The Romans had Philip swear to an alliance that prevented him aiding any invasion of Antiochus, something that Antiochus himself perhaps hoped if not expected would occur in view of the prior friendly agreements of the kings. However, perhaps Antiochus was also glad that Philip would not join him since he would be able to take over the whole of Macedon and Greece from Philip if he won a war with Rome.

Antiochus wintered in Ephesus and then in the spring of 195 launched an invasion of Thrace (Livy 33.38). He advanced into the territory that a century before had belonged to Lysimachus and was claimed by Seleucus after his victory at Corupedium. According to Livy, the threat of Antiochus' forces was enough to compel the surrender of many cities in the region. When he advanced on Lysimachus' old capital of Lysimacheia he found it in ruins and, despairing of its fate, set about rebuilding the city and restoring its inhabitants. In spending time on all these activities, it is clear that Antiochus was not worried at all about any impending Roman intervention.

While Antiochus was in Lysimacheia the Romans sent an embassy to request him to leave Europe (Livy 33.39-40). They requested that he restore to Ptolemy the cities he had newly taken and to hand over to them the cities that had previously had allegiance to Philip. Antiochus countered that he and Ptolemy were now on friendly terms and concluding a marriage alliance. He stated that the Romans should allow him freedom in Asia just as he did not question the Roman moves in Italy. Finally, he insisted that the territory of Lysimachus in Thrace belonged to him through Seleucus I's conquest.

The talks broke off when a rumour of Ptolemy's death circulated and both sides made haste to get to Egypt (Livy 33.41). Antiochus took his fleet via Ephesus to Cyprus. After successfully putting down a mutiny of his soldiers, a huge storm destroyed a large part of his fleet and he returned to Ephesus for the winter. That Ptolemy was still alive prevented Antiochus from taking more Egyptian territory and is probably what turned him onto invading Greece the following spring.

Livy states that the arrival from Carthage of the exiled Hannibal prompted Antiochus into starting a war against Rome (Livy 33.49). However, even after that Livy reports the numerous attempts of Antiochus to obtain an alliance with Rome. The sticking-point was Antiochus' new conquests in Thrace and of Greek cities in Asia Minor (Livy 34.57-9). The Romans claimed to champion Greek freedom after their victory over Philip removed his garrisons in Greek cities. Antiochus' messengers argued that their king was being honourable in only seeking to control areas that Seleucus had conquered and were therefore his by inheritance. The Romans countered that championing Greek freedom was more honourable than returning Greek cities to subservience, even slavery, under a monarch. What is likely is that Antiochus was openly negotiating for peace but secretly preparing for war. Livy confirms in detail his machinations with Hannibal to plan a joint war against Rome (Livy 34.60). Hannibal even sent a messenger, monetarily supported by Antiochus, to Carthage to argue for war jointly with Antiochus. On his pleas failing to move the Carthaginian Senate, who reported events to Rome, the messenger fled, forcing Antiochus to contemplate war with Rome on his own terms (Livy 34.61-2).

However, even after this event Livy emphasizes that it took great persuasion from the Aetolians to finally tempt Antiochus to enter Greece in arms and even then he came much later. The Aetolians, who had first invited Rome into Greece to oppose Philip, tried to stir the three main monarchs in the region to begin a war on Rome: Philip, Antiochus and Nabis the tyrant of Sparta (Livy 35.12). Livy records the deputations sent to each ruler. Nabis quickly followed the Aetolian advice and sought to retake Spartan coastal cities from Roman supporters, but with Philip the Aetolian ambassadors argued that he should go to war because of the extra strength of Antiochus and the presence of Hannibal as a commander. Philip refused. Antiochus accepted the arguments of the

Aetolians but still delayed any action. He went to Syria to celebrate the wedding of his daughter to Ptolemy and then invaded Pisidia in Asia Minor (Livy 35.12). On his return the next spring after the death of his eldest son Antiochus, he welcomed yet more ambassadors from Rome to discuss an alliance (Livy 35.15-7). If he did intend war with Rome, where was the urgency? He most certainly waited until he believed he had the opportune moment. It took four years after the defeat of Philip for Antiochus to finally take the plunge.

After this latest set of negotiations ended in the same stalemate over freedom for Greek cities, according to Livy, Antiochus held a council of war and became set on invading Greece (Livy 35.18), especially after reconciling with Hannibal as his main anti-Rome agitator (Livy 35.19).[1] An Acarnanian in his court, who arrived after Philip's defeat, told him that an invasion of Greece would furnish him with the armies of Philip, Nabis and the Aetolians. This and Hannibal's reaffirmed hatred of Rome instilled in him as a child persuaded Antiochus to this course of action.

Yet while Antiochus delayed, Nabis continued his war in Greece as prompted by the Aetolians the year before (Livy 35.25-30). The longer Antiochus waited, the less likely Nabis would be able to aid a war in Greece. Moreover, while he delayed the Romans prepared for war and sent messengers around the various cities in Greece reaffirming their allegiance to Rome if Antiochus did come.

Unfortunately for Antiochus, Nabis suffered great reverses at the hands of the Achaean League under Philopoemen, arguably the finest Greek general of his generation.[2] The Aetolians tried to counter the Roman messengers and coerce cities into joining them and Antiochus. Their scheme worked at Demetrias in Thessaly, one of the so-called Fetters of Greece (Livy 35.31-4). However, at Sparta, where they tried to replace Nabis with their own tyrant (Livy 35.35-6) Nabis' assassination led to Sparta joining the Achaean League at the advice of Philopoemen (Livy 35.37). It is very clear that Antiochus' inaction and indecisiveness denied him the support of numerous possible allies who may have joined him had he arrived before Rome could undermine his growing influence in certain cities.

Antiochus Finally Arrives in Greece

According to Livy (35.42), it was the Aetolian capture of Demetrias that finally persuaded Antiochus to launch his invasion. However, he was also encouraged by Aetolian lies that a large army of Greeks awaited him. His force of 10,000 infantry, 500 cavalry and 6 elephants was pitifully small (Livy 35.43). Nonetheless, Antiochus persisted with activities against Roman wishes in trying to persuade every Greek city he could to join him. This was the only way his army would increase sufficiently. He still seemed unconcerned about Rome declaring war.

It was Antiochus' own folly that provided the catalyst for the unlooked-for war when his forces routed a small reconnaissance force of Roman soldiers at the sanctuary of Delium, giving the Romans an excuse to declare war (Livy 35.50.7-51.5; Diod. 29.1; App. *Syr.* 15). He may not have sanctioned the attack, as he released all Roman prisoners at Chalcis (Zon. 9.19), but he should have given strict orders to all his men not to engage with Rome unless engaged by them, similar to modern standing orders to fire only when fired upon. Prior to this skirmish both sides had shown repeatedly limited desire for all-out war, though each side's posturing is what led to the conflict. Antiochus should have been more careful, if he truly did not want war, to avoid at all costs provoking the sleeping giant. This was especially true since he did not receive anywhere near enough military support from the Greek states to justify his strong stance in Greece.

He began well by forcing Euboia to come over to him, but once Rome determined to prosecute the war Antiochus had little chance with such a small army. It is clear from Livy that Antiochus' prospects of outside assistance were zero. In fact Philip, Ptolemy, Carthage and Masinissa, the king of Numidia, offered assistance to Rome in the war against Antiochus. The Romans turned down monetary offers from all, and denied the need for military assistance from Ptolemy and a navy from Carthage. However, they did request that Philip send military assistance to their consul in Greece (Livy 36.4).

Hannibal, when finally consulted, offered very sound advice which Antiochus completely ignored. First he argued that Antiochus had to persuade Philip to join him in the war and, if he could not, to distract him by an invasion of Macedon through Antiochus' son Seleucus who had an army in Thrace at Lysimacheia. Following that, he argued for the course of the attack (Livy 36.7):

> As regards the general strategy of the war, you have known from the outset what my views are. Had I been listened to then, it would not have been the capture of Chalcis or the storming of a fort on the Euripus that the Romans would have heard about; they would have learnt that Etruria and Liguria and the coastal districts of Cisalpine Gaul were wrapped in the flames of war and, what would have alarmed them most of all, that Hannibal was in Italy. I am of opinion that even now you ought to bring up the whole of your military and naval forces and let a fleet of transports accompany them laden with supplies. We here are too few for the requirements of war and too many for our scanty commissariat. When you have concentrated your entire strength, Antiochus, you might divide your fleet and keep one division cruising off Corcyra, that there may be no safe and easy passage for the Romans, the other you would send across to the coast of Italy opposite Sardinia and Africa. You yourself would advance with all your land forces into the country round Byllis; from there you would protect Greece and give the Romans the impression that you are going to sail to Italy, and should circumstances render it necessary you will be in readiness to do so.

Hannibal longed for backing to launch another invasion of Italy, but his advice to threaten Italy and at the very least block easy naval crossings was crucial if Antiochus had hopes of delaying Rome from being able to constantly bring reinforcements. However, the most poignant part of his advice is that the army was 'too few for the requirements of war and too many for our scanty commissariat'. In other words, the necessary workings of an army ready to oppose Rome involved a larger number of troops than Antiochus had, and the number of officers he had were too few to successfully organize and command the army that he did have. Hannibal clearly demonstrates his military expertise in this advice and modestly ends his argument by pointing out his own successes:

> This is what I advise you to do, and though I may not be profoundly versed in every phase of war, how to war with the Romans at all

events I have learnt through success and failure alike. In the measures which I have advised you to take I promise to co-operate most loyally and energetically.

Antiochus would have done well had he listened to someone with such a great history of success against Rome. As it was, he ignored the advice and carried on trying desperately, but in vain, to persuade Greek cities to join him. His one slight success was in forcing the cities in Thessaly to his side after he punished the first city of Pherae (Livy 36.9), but Roman forces advised by Philip relieved Larissa and created a dividing line between Antiochus and Roman territory in Thessaly (Livy 36.10).

After both sides retired for winter, during which time Antiochus got married and had no concern for maintaining discipline or order in his troops (Livy 36.11), hostilities resumed in the spring.[3] The Romans and Philip together began successively recapturing Thessalian cities (Livy 36.13-4). After a short time they had managed to capture Antiochus' garrisons numbering 4,000 soldiers from an ally state, Athamania. Since Antiochus had such a small expeditionary force to begin with, the loss of 4,000 troops was a huge blow to his hopes. Moreover, Philip released the Athamanian prisoners home and his arrival in the region persuaded the Athamanian state to abandon Antiochus in favour of Philip and Rome. The Roman reconquest of Thessaly denied Antiochus all his garrison troops. The Roman consul treated the soldiers well; 1,000 of them agreed to serve under Philip and the rest returned to Demetrias without weapons.

Despairing of achieving anything, Antiochus finally realized his position was entirely untenable. He told the Aetolians to meet him for battle and when they came with a small force, Antiochus withdrew to Thermopylae as a fortress of last resort. Livy (36.15) initially does not even provide a total for the number of Aetolian troops who arrived, saying only that the leading men brought a few retainers with them. Later he confirms that 4,000 Aetolians arrived (Livy 36.16). Antiochus now finally realized that the Aetolian promises of aid were lies and according to Livy (36.15) regretted ignoring Hannibal's advice to attack sooner or bring his whole army.

The Battle of Thermopylae

Forced onto the defensive because of his wildly unsuccessful attempts to win over Greece to his leadership, Thermopylae was his only refuge. The small pass at Thermopylae was the easiest of the two routes into Greece from Thessaly and the only one large enough for a significant army to pass. It had long been fortified as a defensive strongpoint. Numerous battles through the centuries occurred at this natural chokepoint, from the most famous action by Leonidas of Sparta to the engagement in the Second World War of retreating Allied ANZAC troops delaying the German invasion of Greece.

I am not entirely sure what Antiochus hoped to achieve by shutting himself in at Thermopylae unless he was buying time for his main army to arrive. There was absolutely no way that he could hope to win the war by sheltering at Thermopylae. Even so, he formidably fortified his camp in the pass to await a Roman attack. Despite his desperation for more soldiers, he sent the Aetolian forces out from this defensive stronghold forward of his position to two cities. There the Aetolians had no hope of doing anything to counter the advance of the Romans. Indeed, they simply withdrew into Heraclea and let the Romans pass. Antiochus asked them to fortify the smaller mountainous passes in his rear but only half of the 4,000 complied. Perhaps this reveals the reason why he sent them away. He likely did not trust all of that force to fight fully in his defence, especially if the situation became dire, and he wanted them out of the way where they could do no internal harm. In a speech of the Roman commander later, Livy (36.17) suggests that the Aetolians demanded to be allowed to defend the two cities and already feuded among themselves.

The troop totals on either side confirm Roman superiority. Appian (*Syrian Wars* 4.17) states that the Romans fielded 20,000 infantry, 2,000 cavalry and a few elephants. Livy states that the Romans had a force of 40,000-45,000 infantry, 3,500 cavalry and 15 elephants (Livy 35.41, 36.1, 36.14.1). Their army was certainly significantly larger than Antiochus' and many were veterans of the Second Macedonian War. Antiochus, it seems, had only 10,000 infantry, 500 cavalry and his 6 elephants. We do not know how many of each unit type he fielded, but the cavalry were probably his personal heavy cavalry guard unit. The infantry contained missile troops and the phalanx. We can only guess at the respective sizes of each, but since the phalanx was the strength of any Seleucid army this must have accounted for the majority. Perhaps 6,000 to 8,000 as phalangites (three or four regiments of 2,000) is a reasonable supposition.

At the battle, Antiochus deployed his army in front of the ramparts in the now familiar order: Macedonian sarissa phalanx in the centre, missile infantry of archers, slingers and javelin men on the left wing in the foothills, elephants slightly advanced on the right with cavalry and other troops behind them.

Both Livy's and Appian's account of the fighting again suggests that the Macedonian sarissa phalanx was getting the better of the Roman infantry (Livy 36.18, Appian, *Syrian Wars* 4.18-9). Livy states that they withdrew to the rampart and used the extra height to thrust down with their long sarissas to great effect. Then soldiers appeared in the rear of Antiochus' army. At first he thought it was the Aetolians. Once the standards revealed that it was a Roman force which had got through the mountain passes supposedly defended by the Aetolians, the entire Seleucid army fled in disorder.

Though we cannot say much about this battle, we can see again the Seleucid reliance on combined arms and the standard deployment. As a comparison, Thermopylae again confirms the likely deployment at Panion of elephants on the flank of the phalanx. If we venture into the realm of possibilities, in my opinion the backward movement of the phalanx to fight from the ramparts is another example of the feigned withdrawal. Antiochus would benefit from drawing in the Romans in the centre so that his elephants and his missile troops on the wings could attack the flanks of the Romans. This would be a better guarantee of victory than simply fighting in a line until the enemy retreated. Such a tactic could not work so well here since the flanks of the Roman legion were not as vulnerable as those of the Egyptian phalanx at Panion. Moreover, the presence of elephants in the Roman line likely prevented Antiochus' animals from getting at the Roman infantry. It is all a moot point anyway since the Roman troops arrived in the rear at the point when Antiochus' phalanx had taken position on the walls. There was not enough time for any tactic of Antiochus to succeed.

Just like at the more famous battle of Leonidas, the action of Philip V in the Second Macedonian War, and the Greek battle against invading Gauls in 279, the enemy outflanked the force defending the pass by crossing through the mountains. Antiochus knew that might happen and yet did not leave enough troops to prevent it. It is amazing that so many generals failed to sufficiently block the other passes to allow them time to win at Thermopylae. The only success was the Greeks during the Lamian War in 323 forcing back the Macedonian assault of Antipater. Antiochus should have known what would happen, and yet…

Combined Arms

Antiochus' main critical error in this campaign in Greece was not bringing enough troops with him initially. As Livy (35.43) states, he brought to Demetrias '10,000 infantry, 500 cavalry and six elephants, a force hardly sufficient for the occupation of Greece, even if there were no troops there, to say nothing of maintaining a war against Rome'.

What Livy states is very true. Antiochus' force was pitifully small. It was no more than an expeditionary army. Gruen (460) rightly states that the 'forces he brought with him had a moral and psychological impact rather than a military one'.[4] Further on (632), 'The Syrian forces he brought with him could not have held even an unresisting Greece and a war on Rome would be unthinkable. Antiochus had come to make a demonstration, not to wage a war.'

Yet Gruen's conclusion that it was to make a demonstration, not war, is not quite true. Antiochus almost certainly expected the Aetolians to furnish him with a significant number of troops since it was they who had invited him to Greece in order 'to overawe Rome and wring concessions from her, concessions for the benefit of Aetolia', but their support was minimal, amounting to just a few thousand volunteers.[5] According to Livy, the Aetolians had the superior cavalry in Greece (Livy 33.7). However, there is no clear evidence from any attested battles that Aetolian cavalry was better than other cavalry of the era. In fact, the retreat of the Aetolian cavalry force at Panion demonstrates that they were not effective in pitched battles.

Livy's statement explains how at Cynoscephalae the Aetolian cavalry detachment saved the Roman forces from a rout at the hands of the Macedonian skirmishers. This seems more like pro-Roman hyperbole from Livy concerning their Aetolian allies to praise their impact at that battle. The Aetolians certainly knew how to blow their own trumpets, as shown by their extremely exaggerated claims to Antiochus to induce his invasion of Greece. They even claimed that they were primarily responsible for Rome's victory over Philip V. Perhaps Livy's statement is a connection to the same pro-Aetolian sentiments possibly through an Aetolian description of the battle. Livy also claims (33.6) that the Aetolians won an earlier cavalry skirmish for Rome. Yet after the Battle of Cynoscephalae, Livy (33.11) mentions that the Roman army commander 'was disgusted with the Aetolians for their insatiable appetite for plunder and their arrogance in claiming for themselves the credit of the victory, a piece of vanity which offended all men's ears'.

There seem to be two strands of analysis of the Aetolians in the Second Macedonian War. One praises the Aetolians for bringing timely aid to Rome, aid that the Romans seemed very keen to secure according to Livy and deserving praise for turning the tide against Philip. The other sees the Romans trying to minimize the Aetolian involvement in the war and keep them in line. Livy states (33.6) that the Roman cavalry superiority was 'owing to the accession of the Aetolians'. Yet the Aetolians furnished only 600 infantry and 400 cavalry (Livy 33.3). That force was hardly the decisive collection of troops in the Roman army. For example, the Athamanians brought 1,200 infantry to the Roman-led coalition. Livy's praise is certainly on Aetolian cavalry throughout, despite their small number. Unfortunately, no source provides a detailed description of the Roman army totals or for the whole cavalry. The only force we hear of is the 400 Aetolians. If the Romans had cavalry superiority, their force must have been more than Philip's 2,000 comprising expert Macedonian and Thessalian horsemen.

Polybius (18.22) provides a more understandable context for where Livy's praise of Aetolian cavalry comes from regarding the action at Cynoscephalae: 'For as much as the Aetolian infantry is inferior in the equipment and discipline required for a general engagement, by so much is their cavalry superior to that of other Greeks in detached and single combats.' It seems likely that Livy has appropriated Polybius' comment and changed the emphasis from 'in detached and single combats' to overall superiority. On the hilly and broken terrain of Cynoscephalae the Aetolian cavalry was in its element. Aetolia is a famously rough hilly region in central Greece. This topography led to Aetolian infantry minimizing hoplites and excelling as light infantry. The same is clearly true of their cavalry. Their horsemen were used to operating in mountainous regions and fighting independently. Other renowned cavalry units such as Macedonian, Thessalian, Achaean, Seleucid or Bactrian primarily excelled in pitched battles on flat ground.

The Aetolian cavalry, then, was not one of the best units of cavalry in Greece as Livy claims. Rather they were the best horsemen when operating on familiar mountainous terrain. This is important to understand why Antiochus should have brought more of his own cavalry with him across the Aegean or down from Thrace. He could even have just brought the cavalry soldiers without their mounts and found horses for them in Thessaly or other areas. That he relied on Aetolia providing him a cavalry unit to protect his phalanx demonstrated his lack of preparation and forethought for his invasion.

Antiochus' expeditionary army was a similar size to the force brought to Italy by Pyrrhus 100 years earlier except that Pyrrhus did gain reinforcements from a large army of locals. Despite their promises, the Aetolians could not furnish anywhere near enough troops to aid Antiochus. This was because of the complete subjugation of Sparta and the refusal of Philip, likely held in check by the fact that the Romans held his son as a hostage for his good behaviour. Antiochus told the Aetolians he intended to bring his full army over in the spring, but the unfavourable season prevented doing so at the time. This was likely true, but the Romans forced him from Greece before this occurred. Hindsight is a wonderful thing, but surely Antiochus would have been advised to wait out the winter and arrive in the spring with his full army. Why he did not do so and trusted the Aetolian promise of troops so much is one of the most important unanswerable questions in Seleucid history.[6]

Antiochus' Strategy and Failings

After his arrival did not prompt enough Greek states to join him and provide reinforcements to bolster his army, Antiochus had two choices: to stay or to leave. If he did intend to fight Rome in Greece he would need more soldiers. If he intended to demonstrate his power to force Greek states to join him as the preserver of Greek freedom he needed to stay in Greece. Both of these options required more soldiers for either war or garrisons. It was clear shortly after he arrived that these troops would not come from any states in Greece.

What is not clear in all of this and yet what is the most important question is exactly why Antiochus did not bring his full army to join him in Greece that spring. He had surely seen in his time in Greece that autumn that he needed his own men. Nowhere near enough Greek states would furnish troops and the force he did bring was inadequate even to defeat the Roman allies in Greece. According to Livy Hannibal told him as much before the winter and yet at the onset of spring he still had no reinforcements and seemingly had not made any preparations to leave.

We are surely missing some information in our sources that can explain this delay. Antiochus in his meeting with the Aetolians had promised to bring his full army and yet they did not arrive. Perhaps Roman actions in the early spring of 192 were so successful that Antiochus had to wait for his full army. It would take time for the army to be ready to sail across the Aegean Sea or to march around through Thrace, time that Antiochus did not have.

In my view, his defensive stance at Thermopylae was to buy time for his main army to arrive later in the year. Antiochus knew in hindsight that he should have brought over the army before the winter or even have come with them at the very start. To leave would be to abandon for good the whole concept of defending Greek freedoms and his ambitions to control an empire to rival Alexander the Great. He had to stay, but he knew he did not have the army to fight the Romans in battle or even to avoid battle and gain cities instead. Strategically there was nothing to gain from holding Thermopylae instead of leaving Greece unless he needed to delay the Roman army long enough for reinforcements to arrive. We know that he could expect no such reinforcements from anywhere in Greece, so it must have been his army in Thrace or Asia.

As further proof of this all the battles fought at Thermopylae through the centuries were between a local Greek army seeking to delay an invading force. The only reason to fight at Thermopylae was to defend access into Greece from the north. Antiochus was too experienced a commander not to know that without reinforcements he had no hope of defeating the Roman army. He held the pass to delay the Romans for long enough for aid to come and hopefully allow him to go on the offensive later in the season. Unfortunately, he could not hold the pass and so fled ignominiously.

For four years after the end of the Second Macedonian War Antiochus had delayed from actually invading Greece, and longer if he had ever intended to come to help Philip before he lost his own war with Rome. That inaction should have led to preparing an invading army if he was serious about taking on Rome. Yet when he did finally arrive, our sources suggest he came almost on a whim, persuaded finally by empty Aetolian promises, bringing only a scratch force of his personal troops.

In hindsight, Antiochus should have committed to an invasion of Greece immediately after his successful conclusion to his war against Egypt when he had finally conquered Coele-Syria. Then in 198 Philip had begun to lose the upper hand over Rome. At that time perhaps Philip did not want assistance, but he made peace overtures to Rome the following winter (198/7), so he may have been willing to accept Antiochus' help. Livy (35.18) states that one of Antiochus' officers, a defector from Philip, recalled 'how often during the war Philip had besought all the gods to give him the help of Antiochus; if this prayer were now granted he would not lose an hour in recommencing war'.

Certainly before he finally signed a treaty with Rome to end the war in 196, Philip likely would have accepted Antiochus' assistance in trying to win the Second Macedonian War, though the sources do not state that he ever asked as much. Just as Hannibal argued in Livy later, had Antiochus joined with Philip together they had a chance of defeating Rome, especially if Nabis had joined them. This is what the Aetolian ambassadors argued would happen, but their embassy had argued that in 194 before Nabis' defeat and before Philip had time to enjoy friendly relations with Rome after the treaty. By 192 circumstances were completely different and entirely unfavourable.

The year 196 was when such a confluence of actors could have joined together in concert against Rome, and many Greek states may have joined them. Moreover, in 196 Antiochus had successfully invaded Thrace and founded Lysimacheia, so he already had an easy route to continue into Greece. The Romans realized this too when they sent commissioners to meet Antiochus in Thrace. That conference was enough to turn Antiochus away from continuing to Greece and lose his greatest opportunity of victory.

What is more likely is that Antiochus had no initial intention of actually invading Greece. He seemed for the next few years perfectly happy securing territory in Asia Minor and Thrace and extending his kingdom to the same size as that of Seleucus I before his assassination. The Romans also seemed happy to avoid war with Antiochus, giving him many chances to stay in Asia, even at the end allowing him to keep Asia Minor. However, since Antiochus determined to hold onto his gains in Thrace, war was inevitable. Antiochus must have known that from the Roman insistence. As it was, Antiochus delayed for too many years, lost the opportune moment and arrived with no great fanfare and then left Greece in complete ignominy.

The turning-point in Antiochus' intentions was the Aetolian seizure of Demetrias. Control of this fortress in Thessaly finally persuaded Antiochus that he would gain Greece without much fighting now Rome had left the area entirely. As Rosenstein states:[7]

> And when an Aetolian force treacherously seized the city of Demetrias, one of the strategic Three Fetters, and then informed Antiochus that the town had spontaneously revolted from the Romans and gone over to his side, the king was convinced that he would everywhere be welcomed as a liberator.

Antiochus was so enamoured with the Aetolian arguments that he completely disregarded the prior Roman threats. He and his advisors must have known that Rome would answer his invasion with a substantial army, just as Hannibal argued in the Seleucid army conference in Greece. Maybe Antiochus did not think a Roman army would arrive as fast as it did. This is perhaps why his main army never followed him to Greece. He certainly believed that most Greek states would join him immediately upon his arrival with a purely demonstrative force. Maybe he did believe that Nabis or Philip would join him. Few other Greek states had enough manpower to sufficiently increase his army to the required level to face Rome. Without those two as allies, it is difficult to understand how else Antiochus intended to build his army from the 12,000 he brought to the 30,000 he would need. Unfortunately, all his hopes were in vain.

Whatever the truth of the matter, Antiochus' actions in this disastrous invasion of Greece demonstrate just how negligent or overconfident he was as a commander and how unaware he was of crucial political happenings. Despite his successes in the previous decades, Antiochus' generalship in this instance was significantly less than average. As a result, he started a war in Greece that he had little chance of winning and that would have dire repercussions throughout the East.

After Thermopylae Antiochus rode for his life with his 500 cavalry eventually reaching Chalcis, the site of his winter marriage, and sailed for home. The Romans captured the entirety of the rest of his army, more than 10,000 men according to our sources.

Thus ended Antiochus' ignominious invasion of Greece. It was nothing short of an unmitigated disaster. He achieved nothing except starting a war with Rome and gained nothing except a new wife. He lost more than 10,000 soldiers, the respect of Hannibal and any strategic advantage over the Romans. It was only a matter of time before Rome brought the war into Asia to punish Antiochus and he could do absolutely nothing but wait and gather his forces.

Figure 13. Early coin before Molon.

SELEUKID EMPIRE. Antiochos III 'the Great'. 222-187 bc. AR Tetradrachm (25.9mm, 16.92g, 1h). Alexandrine types struck in the name of Antiochos. Susa mint. Struck 223–222 bc (first reign, before Molon). Head of Herakles right, wearing lion skin/Zeus Aëtophoros seated left; monogram in left field and below throne. SC 1205, ESM 379, HGC 9, 445. VF, lightly toned, light marks and scratches, struck from a worn obverse die. (*Source: Classical Numismatic Group, LLC* https://www.cngcoins.com/Coin.aspx?CoinID=360429)

Figure 14. Coin after Molon.

SELEUKID KINGS of SYRIA. Antiochos III (the Great). 223–187 BC. AR Tetradrachm (28mm, 16.73g). Susa mint. Struck during second reign at Susa, 220–187 BC. Diademed head right, with small horn/Apollo seated left on omphalos, holding arrow and resting hand on bow; monograms in outer left and right fields. SC 1214.2; Le Rider, *Suse* 38; cf. SNG Spaer 764. VF, cleaned and a bit bright.

The small horn on the head of Antiochos that makes its appearance on this and other concurrent issues commemorates Antiochos' suppression of the usurper Molon in Susa. (*Source: Classical Numismatic Group, LLC* https://www.cngcoins.com/Coin.aspx?CoinID=51706#)

Figure 15. Coin with elephant.

Houghton 42. Antiochos III AR Drachm. Nisibis mint. Struck circa 205–200 BC. Diademed head right/ΒΑΣΙΛΕΩΣ above, ΑΝΤΙΟΧΟΥ below, elephant walking right; monogram before.

antiochos_III/Houghton_0042. (*With permission of wildwinds.com, ex CNG Auction 1999*)

Figure 16. Coin with Athena and Nike.

Houghton 492. Antiochos III, Seleukid Kingdom, AE20, 222–187 BC. 5.90g. Uncertain mint '62' in Southern Coele, Syria. Struck 198–187 BC. Helmeted head of Athena right/ΒΑΣΙΛΕΩΣ ΑΝΤΙΟΧΟΥ to right and left of Nike standing left, holding wreath and palm branch, anchor above ΠΑ monogram in left field. Hoover HGC 492; SC 1095.4 var. (monogram).

antiochos_III/Hoover_492. (*With permission of wildwinds.com, ex cngcoins.com, auction 421 (2018)*)

Figure 17. The author holding an 18ft-long sarissa made by students in an experiential history class.

Figure 18. The author and students marching with sarissas over a ditch.

Figure 19. The author's students in a static phalanx unit of two ranks of seven (the historical unit was ranks of eight).

Figure 20. The author's students in a static phalanx unit of 4 × 3.

Figure 21. The author's students jovially recreating attacking a Roman legionary: the legionary perspective.

Figure 22. The author's students jovially recreating attacking a Roman legionary: the phalanx perspective.

Chapter Five

The Legion versus the Phalanx: Roman and Macedonian Styles of Warfare

Before we move on to the final confrontation between Antiochus and Rome at Magnesia ad Sipylum we need to examine the different styles of warfare of Rome and the Macedonians and Greeks. Without going into detailed analysis of the battles of the Second Macedonian War or later conflicts, we can look at the basics.

Polybius (18.28-32) provides a detailed analysis from his biased perspective of the relative strengths and weaknesses of the two styles of battle so this is a good place to start with a brief subsequent analysis of his main points.

Polybius is clear that the strength of the phalanx is its frontal attack: 'When the phalanx has its characteristic virtue and strength nothing can sustain its frontal attack or withstand the charge as can easily be understood for many reasons.' The reasons he gives are primarily the length of the sarissas allowing five blades to protrude before the first rank, and the tightness of the formation allowing those behind to add impetus to those in front. I have discussed all these strengths in the Introduction.

What is of more interest here is how and why the advancing phalanx holds advantages over the Roman legion:

Now in the case of the Romans also each soldier with his arms occupies a space of three feet in breadth, but as in their mode of fighting each man must move separately, as he has to cover his person with his long shield, turning to meet each expected blow, and as he uses his sword both for cutting and thrusting it is obvious that a looser order is required, and each man must be at a distance of at least three feet from the man next him in the same rank and those in front of and behind him, if they are to be of proper use. The consequence will be that one Roman must stand opposite two men in the first rank of the phalanx, so that he has to face and encounter ten pikes, and it is both impossible for a single man to cut through them all in time once they are at close quarters and by no means easy to force their points away, as the rear ranks can be of no help to the front rank either in thus forcing the pikes away or in the use of the sword. So it is easy to see that, as I said at the beginning, nothing can withstand the charge of the phalanx as long as it preserves its characteristic formation and force.

Polybius clearly analyses the difference between the two heavy infantry units. The phalanx relies on its huge spear and tight formation whereas the Roman soldier fights with the famous gladius short sword that is equally adept in thrusting or slashing. As he emphasizes, the long sarissa that causes such distance between the front ranks of each soldier makes the difference. Each Roman soldier has to use their short sword to try to get past five sarissas before he can get at the actual body of the front-rank soldier of the phalanx. This difference is insurmountable for Romans with swords so long as the phalanx stays in formation.

Polybius goes on:

What then is the reason of the Roman success, and what is it that defeats the purpose of those who use the phalanx? It is because in war the time and place of action is uncertain and the phalanx has only one time and one place in which it can perform its peculiar service. Now, if the enemy were obliged to adapt themselves to the times and places required by the phalanx when a decisive battle was impending, those who use the phalanx would in all probability, for the reasons I stated above, always get the better of their enemies; but if it is not only possible but easy to avoid its onset why should one any longer dread an attack of a body so constituted? Again, it is acknowledged that the phalanx requires level and clear ground with no obstacles such as ditches, clefts, clumps of trees, ridges and water courses, all of which are sufficient to impede and break up such a formation.

In summary, Polybius makes the now standard argument that the phalanx is incapable of functioning on difficult terrain. On anything other than flat ground, the phalanx will break apart and is unable to overcome obstacles in its path. He then argues that it is impossible to find many places where flat terrain is open enough for a phalanx:

> Everyone would also acknowledge that it is almost impossible except in very rare cases to find spaces of say twenty stades or even more in length with no such obstacles. But even if we assume it to be possible, supposing those who are fighting against us refuse to meet us on such ground, but force round sacking the cities and devastating the territory of our allies, what is the use of such a formation? For by remaining on the ground that suits it, not only is it incapable of helping its friends but cannot even ensure its own safety. For the arrival of supplies will easily be prevented by the enemy, when they have undisturbed command of the open country.

He argues that limited suitable terrain opens up the enemy to have free rein to attack cities or harass the collection of supplies or allies because the phalanx will be unable to fight in those locations. Then he continues with how the Roman army is able to successfully oppose the phalanx head-on:

> But if the phalanx leaves the ground proper to it and attempts any action, it will be easily overcome by the enemy. And again, if it is decided to engage the enemy on level ground, but instead of availing ourselves of our total force when the phalanx has its one opportunity for charging, we keep out of action even a small portion of it at the moment of the shock, it is easy to tell what will happen from what the Romans always do at present, the likelihood of the result I now indicate requiring no argument but only the evidence of actual facts.

By compelling the phalanx to move off level ground, or by only committing a small section of the total force to battle with the phalanx, the Roman soldiers are able to attack the phalanx when it is vulnerable, on the flanks or if its formation breaks up. The Romans are able to do so better than most infantry units because of the more open formation they utilize:

For the Romans do not make their line equal in force to the enemy and expose all the legions to a frontal attack by the phalanx, but part of their forces remain in reserve and the rest engage the enemy. Afterwards whether the phalanx drives back by its charge the force opposed to it or is repulsed by this force, its own peculiar formation is broken up. For either in following up a retreating foe or in flying before an attacking foe, they leave behind the other parts of their own army, upon which the enemy's reserve have room enough in the space formerly held by the phalanx to attack no longer in front but appearing by a lateral movement on the flank and rear of the phalanx.

So, according to Polybius, when the phalanx advances through success or retreats through defeat gaps appear either in the phalanx formation itself or on its flanks between any supporting units. Both such instances are indeed devastating to a phalanx as its entire strength rests in it maintaining an unbroken formation as discussed in the Introduction.

For Polybius this easy exposure of the phalanx's vulnerable flanks makes the Roman formation superior: 'When it is thus easy to guard against the opportunities and advantages of the phalanx, but impossible to prevent the enemy from taking advantage of the proper moment to act against it, the one kind of formation naturally proves in reality superior to the other.'

Polybius is clear that it was simple to expose the frailties of the phalanx in battle. His analysis continues in this vein. He argues that the phalanx soldiers are of no use completing the other tasks of war, specifically foraging, making and guarding a camp, defending and attacking fortifications, and launching ambuscades. This is because they need the protection of the phalanx, whereas the Roman soldiers are experienced at fighting on their own or in any different formations and circumstances:

Again, those who employ the phalanx have to march through and encamp in every variety of country; they are compelled to occupy favourable positions in advance, to besiege certain positions and to be besieged in others, and to meet attacks from quarters the least expected. For all such contingencies are parts of war, and victory sometimes wholly and sometimes very largely depends on them. Now in all these matters the Macedonian formation is at times of little use and at times of no use at all, because the phalanx soldier can be of service neither in detachments nor singly, while the Roman formation is efficient. For every Roman soldier, once he is armed and sets about his business, can adapt himself equally well to every place and time and can meet attack from every quarter. He is likewise equally prepared and equally in condition whether he has to fight together with the whole army or with a part of it or in maniples or singly.

Polybius concludes his analysis that there is no contest. The Roman formation and soldiers are better in every way than the sarissa phalanx:

So since in all particulars the Romans are much more serviceable, Roman plans are much more apt to result in success than those of others. I thought it necessary to speak on this subject at some length because many Greeks on the actual occasions when the Macedonians suffered defeat considered the event as almost incredible, and many will still continue to wonder why and how the phalanx comes to be conquered by troops armed in the Roman fashion.

Polybius seems shocked that Greeks could not believe or understand why the Romans defeated the Macedonian-style army so often, but in an analysis of his main points we can see that his comparison is not as simple as it sounds and as scholars have hitherto accepted.

Flaws in Polybius' Arguments

Let us deal with each topic in turn:

1. 'It is acknowledged that the phalanx requires level and clear ground with no obstacles such as ditches, clefts, clumps of trees, ridges and water courses, all of which are sufficient to impede and break up such a formation.' (18.31)

The phalanx only functions on flat terrain. Polybius is very clear as the basis for his whole argument that the phalanx formation cannot work on rough or obstructed terrain.

However, this is not necessarily true. There are numerous examples throughout its history of the phalanx not only fighting on rough terrain but actually winning battles over such terrain. Without time to go into detailed analysis of each, a few examples show the need for flat ground for a sarissa phalanx is simply untrue.

Ditches and Water Courses

Alexander the Great won battles at both the Granicus and at Issus when leading his men not only across a river but also up a riverbank that was in places completely impassable. At the Granicus, his cavalry forced a bridgehead to make time for the sarissa phalanx, but Arrian's description clearly demonstrates how the length of the sarissa could clear the riverbank of the enemy enough to allow the soldiers to climb up while maintaining formation.[1] At Issus the bank was so difficult that in one place it did leave a significant gap in the line through which a large force of Greek hoplites fighting for the Persians escaped to the rear. Such was the carnage in the phalanx that according to Arrian the Greeks killed the regimental commander and more than 120 important Macedonians (probably officers or NCOs), but the unmatched difficulty of the terrain and the fight in the resultant gaps did not bring about the defeat of the phalanx.[2]

At Heraclea, his first battle with Rome, Pyrrhus' sarissa phalanx fought ably to defend the riverbank and prevent the Roman forces crossing the River Siris. Pyrrhus' phalanx only fell back initially when Roman cavalry crossed the river elsewhere and threatened the rear of his position. Yet after holding off the cavalry with a desperate heavy cavalry charge, Pyrrhus' phalanx once again defended the uneven terrain of the riverbank and held their position throughout.[3] Even when the soldiers in the phalanx wavered when they believed Pyrrhus had died and gaps began to appear, Pyrrhus' return refortified their resolve and the phalanx remained impenetrable to the Roman attack. Pyrrhus' phalanx showed conclusively that the phalanx formation could very ably fight on the rough terrain of a riverbank, complete with bushes, rocks, little ditches and everything else normally found on the side of a river.

The examples also come from later Hellenistic battles. In the Second Macedonian War, the phalanx of Philip V caused carnage at the River Aous, only fleeing when a relief force of Romans attacked the rear of their position.[4] Polybius himself (4.64.3-11) describes Philip V marching his elite heavy infantry unit, his peltasts, over a river and fighting off an enemy attack. At the Battle of Mantineia in 207 Philopoemen apparently defended his position against Sparta with a ditch.[5] His sarissa phalanx successfully attacked the Spartan formation as it tried to cross the ditch. Yet rather than proving that a ditch prevented a sarissa phalanx from crossing, it shows that it gave the advantage to the defenders attacking with sarissas from a height. Had the Spartan commander Machanidas or any of his subordinate officers viewed the obstacle as impassable, he would not have sent his phalanx to cross it. Perhaps if the soldiers defending the ditch fought with swords, as did the Romans, against the oncoming sarissas of the phalanx the length of the sarissas would have pushed them back, just as at Issus and the Granicus.

Ridges and Hillsides

It was not just rivers over which the phalanx could fight successfully. At Cynoscephalae in 196, the first battle that saw a Roman victory over the phalanx, one wing of the Macedonian phalanx charged down a significant hill with success. Such a hill was far from flat and unimpeded, as Hammond's survey of the site demonstrates.[6] The Romans won because they were able to outflank the phalanx easily when the left wing of the Macedonian army did not reach the battlefield on time or in formation and there was no other unit acting as flank protection.

The Battle of Sellasia best exemplifies how well a phalanx could fight up and downhill.[7] Cleomenes' Spartan phalanx defended a position on a mountainous hillside, and the allied army, ably led by Antigonus and Philopoemen, successfully attacked up the slopes at Cleomenes' position. Cleomenes stationed his army on the summit of two hills separated by a shallow river and the road that followed the valley. He had his men fortify both hills with ramparts created from what was around. Antigonus faced the prospect of marching his phalanx up not one but two hills into the expected shower of missiles as well as following a river in the valley.

The hill on the Spartan left flank was more precipitous than the other so Cleomenes stationed fewer soldiers there under the command of his brother Eucleidas. Antigonus decided to send his best troops up this steep and difficult hill to attack the fortifications at the top. His elite unit of heavy infantry was called the Bronze Shields. As discussed above, these elite units could fight with spear and shield or sarissa and took on all the most difficult military tasks. Antigonus expected the phalanx to be unable to maintain formation in crossing the difficult ground. To mitigate this he stationed between each battalion of the phalanx troops more mobile units of Illyrian light infantry. These troops allowed the line to remain unbroken as different units covered the ground at different paces. Antigonus also hid light infantry in a dry riverbed behind the steeper hill and these troops began the battle with a surprise flanking assault up the hill. This attack bought crucial time for the adapted phalanx to move up the steep slopes.

The articulated phalanx did manage to maintain its formation as it climbed the hillside, showing that a good general could mitigate for a phalanx fighting on very difficult terrain. The only problem came when the centre of the Macedonian army in the valley did not advance to maintain connection to the left flank of the advancing phalanx. Spartan light infantry took advantage of the gap that appeared to attack the flanks and rear of the phalanx causing great carnage. Philopoemen commanding an allied force of Achaean cavalry in the centre asked for permission to counterattack but his commander refused. Insubordinately he sought volunteers and then plunged into the rear of the attacking Spartan light troops. Saved from disaster, the Macedonian phalanx proceeded up the hill and successfully routed the Spartans at the top despite the presence of the fortifications.

This action on the Macedonian right wing shows just how well a phalanx could fight up a rough hillside while under fire. It also shows the vulnerability of its flanks as Polybius obsesses over, but in a combined arms army the other units protect this to great effect as did Philopoemen. Admittedly, against Roman infantry the light Illyrian troops would not have stood up to Roman attacks and would likely have fled, exposing the phalanx's flanks. Yet the point is valid that the terrain itself did not prevent the phalanx ascending the steep slope.

On the other side of the battle Cleomenes with his best troops waited at the top of the hill for Antigonus. The latter had doubled the depth of his phalanx to thirty-two ranks to enable it to maintain its formation climbing the slopes. However, Antigonus, employing the standard Macedonian tactic of holding back the left flank, waited patiently only a short distance from the Spartan lines while his elite forces on the right wing overcame the enemy. Cleomenes saw the writing on the wall as Philopoemen's charge precipitated the rout of his army. He ordered his troops to dismantle the fortifications and charge headlong down the hill straight into Antigonus' waiting phalanx. Antigonus' force initially fell back under the charge, but utilizing its depth it recovered and forced the Spartan phalanx to break and run.

That Cleomenes' sarissa phalanx could charge straight down the hill shows how little the terrain hindered a downhill attack of the phalanx. Far from the formation itself causing gaps to appear in the phalanx on difficult terrain, at Sellasia the phalanxes of both sides proved very capable of attacking uphill or charging downhill.

Clumps of Trees
So of Polybius' list of 'ditches, clefts, clumps of trees, ridges and water courses', the only terrain of which there is no example of a successful phalanx deployment is in clumps of trees. The most famous occasion of a phalanx going through a forest was Pyrrhus' night march at Beneventum.[8] Though it was unsuccessful and Pyrrhus lost the ensuing battle, it was not because of the forest. His problems came from not knowing the right path at night and launching the battle when his men were already exhausted. That Pyrrhus was able to lead a phalanx through the forest shows that it was not an impediment for marching, only for deploying a phalanx.

Indeed, fighting in a forest was beyond the capacity of a sarissa phalanx or any phalanx formation, but that does not mean it was beyond the scope of a Macedonian or Greek soldier. This is the crucial piece of information omitted by Polybius. Macedonian infantry did not only use the sarissa in battle. When the occasion demanded, phalangites would use a spear and shield in the traditional Greek hoplite style. In fact, this method of armament was the standard equipment for most elite heavy infantry regiments in Macedonian-style armies. Alexander's hypaspists, the Hellenistic Argyraspids (or Silver Shields), the Bronze Shields and Antiochus' and Philip V's peltasts all fought with shield and spear just as often as sarissa. Using a spear, Macedonian soldiers could fight adeptly in a forest. Alexander the Great fought numerous engagements among trees supported by his elite heavy infantry and I am sure the scarcity of our sources denied other examples from less well-documented campaigns.

Even if we accept the argument of scholars that Alexander's phalanx was so much better trained than that of those opposing the Romans, Polybius' argument is that the sarissa phalanx formation itself is flawed. He does not state that the phalanx lost to the Romans because its soldiers were less well-trained. He argues that the phalanx itself cannot fight on difficult terrain. Yet, as demonstrated above, there are numerous examples of the phalanx formation working well on difficult terrain and winning battles. What Polybius and other scholars do not appreciate well enough is that the phalanx can fight on difficult terrain as long as the combined arms nature of the army and the tactics of the general ensure the protection of the flanks of the phalanx. That is the whole point of combined arms.

The sarissa phalanx absolutely requires flank support for it to function in any battle scenario. As discussed in the Introduction, all armies since the invention of the sarissa phalanx utilized combined arms. In the fourth century under Philip II, Alexander and the Successors, the strength of the cavalry forces allowed them to use the hammer-and-anvil tactics correctly while still being able to protect the phalanx. By the time of the Roman wars against Macedonian-style armies generals had begun to neglect the other units in favour of the phalanx, forgetting that the one needs the other to function well. Philip V fielded only 2,000 cavalry at Cynoscephalae and, unsurprisingly, the Romans found it very easy to expose the flanks of his unprotected phalanx. Perseus of Macedon did not even have his cavalry fight in the disastrous Battle of Pydna in 167.[9] Antiochus was the exception. He fielded great cavalry and had enough flank protection for the phalanx. As we shall see, lack of support was not the reason for his defeat at Magnesia; how he used that support was the problem.

So, regarding Polybius' first criticism, rough terrain was not by itself an impediment to the phalanx. It only proved disastrous if other units could not protect the flanks and rear of the phalanx. The most successful armies fighting on rough terrain employed combined arms successfully to protect the phalanx. The armies that lost on similar ground when the phalanx was exposed did not. The most famous examples of these defeats are against the Romans at Cynoscephalae and Pydna where neither Macedonian king utilized enough cavalry or other units to prevent a disastrous Roman flank attack on the phalanx.

2. 'Every one would also acknowledge that it is almost impossible except in very rare cases to find spaces of say twenty stades or even more in length with no such obstacles.' (18.31)

Polybius continues his over-emphasized argument about flat terrain by stating that it is impossible to find enough flat terrain for a phalanx to fight meaningful battles in a campaign. Here, there are obvious rebuttals. Throughout history invading armies can rarely conclude a campaign without having to face the enemy army at some point. Even in modern manoeuvre wars, eventually the two sides come together for massed confrontation.

Trying to defend or conquer any territory while avoiding a pitched battle becomes difficult. Either the enemy forces can get behind and threaten avenues of retreat, communication or supply, or local populations will not surrender or switch sides if they know that the enemy force is still around unchecked. In both instances an army reliant on a phalanx can still operate, sending troops in small detachments to block passes, protect or threaten supply lines, or relieve pressure on local areas. There are many instances of actions such as these, even if we only examine the campaigns of Alexander the Great. As argued above, for sarissa phalangites such small-scale deployments usually involve arming with spear and shield, not sarissa, to allow for easier movement and individual fighting styles.

In any campaign one side eventually forces the other to accept a pitched battle to decide the outcome of the war. Indeed most campaigns in the Greek world functioned with the express purpose of forcing the enemy to give battle. The Spartan occupation of the fort in Decelea during the Peloponnesian War intended to force the Athenians outside the walls to fight a battle. The fact that Athenian forces relied on their hide-and-raid strategy prolonged the war, but handed over to Sparta complete control of the local farmland. Usually cities did not want to completely abandon their crops nor did they have the resources as did Athens to import food for their population instead.

So Polybius' argument here is wrong on both fronts. Even though there are limited areas flat enough for a phalanx to fight, a general could easily force the enemy army to fight on just such a purposely-selected flat battlefield by disrupting the flow of the campaign. Throughout Greek and Hellenistic history armies fought battles on the one flat location because they had no other choice. That is why multiple battles in Greece over the centuries took place in the same location. Mantinea, Cynoscephalae and Coronea all saw major battles fought in the same location many centuries apart.

However, Greek history saw hundreds of pitched battles fought in different places that never saw conflict again. If there were so few sites suitable for the phalanx, all battles would take place on these same few sites over and over again. That does not happen because, contrary to Polybius' belief, the phalanx was able to function perfectly well on other types of terrain.

3. 'The arrival of supplies will easily be prevented by the enemy, when they have undisturbed command of the open country.' (18.31)

His main conclusion is that the phalanx cannot protect its supply lines if it waits on good ground. Polybius' whole argument assumes that the army only contains a sarissa phalanx and sits on a patch of flat ground for a whole campaign until the enemy come to offer battle. That is obviously far from the truth. No army ever fielded only a sarissa phalanx. They also included cavalry and light infantry even if sometimes only in small numbers. The main role of these troops in an army was precisely to protect supply lines and hopefully provoke the enemy into offering battle at a site favourable for victory.

In fact, Philip V's first confrontation with Flaminius at Lyncus shows that the phalangites were able to forage properly but the cavalry protected the supply and scouted for the enemy (Livy 31.33). There, the Roman cavalry just about bested the Macedonian horsemen, providing a forewarning of the disaster at Cynoscephalae when the Macedonian cavalry was overpowered and unable to protect the phalanx.

Obviously when foraging the phalangite did not use a sarissa but a spear, if he was armed at all. Most likely the light infantry present in the army would do most of the foraging as they were particularly well suited to ranging over any terrain, but if an army required large quantities of supplies then the heavy infantry would do so too. The cavalry would protect everyone.

Polybius' arguments are only relevant if the Macedonian army consisted only of soldiers from the phalanx armed with just a sarissa. Only in this case would such soldiers be unable to forage, protect their supply lines or scout for the enemy, or even do anything that an army must do. This is clearly far from the truth, and most of the jobs done outside of a battle could be and were accomplished by light infantry or cavalry.

Foraging was usually carried out by the light infantry, but if soldiers of the phalanx had to do it they would simply gather supplies unarmed or using their spears and defensive swords protected by the cavalry. Polybius is right that it is impossible to gather supplies while armed with a sarissa or in a phalanx, but no general in his right mind would try to do such a thing.

4. 'If the phalanx leaves the ground proper to it and attempts any action, it will be easily overcome by the enemy. And again, if it is decided to engage the enemy on level ground, but instead of availing ourselves of our total force when the phalanx has its one opportunity for charging, we keep out of action even a small portion of it at the moment of the shock, it is easy to tell what will happen…. For the Romans do not make their line equal in force to the enemy and expose all the legions to a frontal attack by the phalanx, but part of their forces remain in reserve and the rest engage the enemy.' (18.31-2)

The phalanx is easy to overcome when it is not fighting on level ground or by keeping in reserve some soldiers not engaged with the phalanx in the centre.

Finally, Polybius provides an argument of successful tactics in overcoming a phalanx. He is of course right, as is obvious to anyone, that the phalanx is vulnerable on its flanks if they are exposed. He is also right that if gaps appear in the front of the phalanx Roman infantry armed with short swords can get inside the reach of the sarissas and cause absolute carnage. He suggests that the Romans succeed easily because their formation allows them to hold troops back from engaging with the phalanx in the centre. These troops can then redeploy to attack the phalanx on its flanks.

The Roman formation was the chequerboard system of maniples. A maniple was a unit of Roman infantry numbering around 120 soldiers. According to the surviving military manuals describing Hellenistic armies, after the wars with Rome the Macedonian-style phalanx adopted the unit of 120 as the lowest self-contained unit in a regiment to which the messengers and standard-bearers attached. There is even evidence in both Xenophon and the tactical manuals that through training the hoplite or sarissa phalanx could also fight in a chequerboard formation.[10]

Roman legions combined four different types of infantry. The velites were the light infantry using javelins and other missiles. The hastati were armoured light infantry still reliant on a javelin but able to use shields and swords to engage in hand-to-hand combat if necessary. These were the Roman equivalent of Classical Greek peltasts. The next unit was the principes. These were hardened well-armed heavy infantry soldiers who threw javelins to begin with and then fought in close quarters with swords. The final unit was the veteran spearmen of the triarii. These soldiers could close up and fight as a shield wall or tight phalanx.

Aside from the velites, each of these unit types deployed in maniples. The hastati and principes numbered 120 soldiers per maniple, the triarii closer to 60. The velites fought in open order as befitted their role as light infantry skirmishers. The maniples of the various units took up positions leaving the space of a maniple between each maniple.[11] This formation is what made it look like a chequerboard from above.

In battles, the Romans kept their best veteran troops as their rearmost lines. This allowed the veterans to support where needed most in the fighting. The valuable experience of the veteran troops was not wasted in the front lines of the battle until needed to turn the tide. This strategy kept the veterans alive longer and thus kept the most effective and best troops out of danger to use elsewhere. It also allowed the younger troops to gain much-needed experience. It was a sort of trial by combat where those who survived and excelled in the younger units would graduate to the veteran positions and earn their respite in the rear of the formation.

This tactic of having veterans fight in the rear was different from most militaries in the ancient world. In most other cultures it was a point of pride for the best soldiers to fight in the front ranks and prove their superiority. In the Greek phalanx the best troops always fought in the front ranks so as to provide a cutting edge and do the most damage to the enemy. Of course, it also meant that most of the casualties in a battle came among the best veteran troops in those front ranks. Numerous Greek generals and kings died fighting gloriously in the front ranks, most notably the great Epaminondas and the Spartan King Agis III, at Mantineia and Megalopolis respectively. Eventually losing the best troops over and over again denuded a state of its best soldiers, as Carthage discovered during the Punic Wars. Rome kept more veteran soldiers alive and allowed newer soldiers to gain experience faster. With a significantly reduced drain of veteran troops, Roman armies proved that much more effective in wars over a longer period.

So the Roman system did indeed allow more flexibility of deployment on the battlefield. Roman soldiers could stand back from the sarissa points of the phalanx and bide their time until it was safer to strike. If terrain did open gaps in the front, the Romans could commit more men to the front. If the flanks became exposed they could attack there. Moreover, the javelins of the velites, hastati and principes would do some damage against the soldiers of the phalanx while holding back. However, waiting and holding back from the phalanx only works if it then becomes possible to attack its vulnerable points.

As discussed at length above, the sarissa phalanx can only function properly and effectively in an army making good use of combined arms. Only if other units protect its flanks sufficiently can the phalanx succeed in overcoming the enemy in the centre. This is what occurred in all the major victories of the Hellenistic phalanx. Chaeronea, Issus, Gaugamela, Heraclea, Raphia, Sellasia and Panion all saw the phalanx hold the centre of the field ably protected on its flanks. The role of the phalanx as the anvil was to hold the centre while other units attacked elsewhere and drove the enemy onto the hedge of the waiting sarissas. The list of battles of a successful hammer-and-anvil attack includes almost every battle the sarissa phalanx ever fought, but the notable absences of such a tactic at Cynoscephalae, Magnesia and Pydna are not surprisingly the three most famous battles where Rome defeated the phalanx.

At Heraclea, Pyrrhus proved that the Roman legion was vulnerable to the phalanx if it maintained formation and other units attacked the enemy on the wings, thus protecting its flanks. Even in defeat at Beneventum the phalanx held its own and the loss came when the elephants ran amok. As I argue elsewhere,[12] elephants are not suited to charging the enemy but rather holding a flank. The phalanx of Philip V at the River Aous and Atrax and Antiochus at Thermopylae easily repulsed numerous Roman attacks despite the Romans fighting in maniples and holding men back from the centre.

The defeats suffered by the phalanx at Cynoscephalae, Magnesia and Pydna came about not because the Roman formation was inherently superior as Polybius claims. Rather poor generalship in each case denied the phalanx the necessary flank protection of other units. At Cynoscephalae Philip V had sent his light infantry and cavalry ahead keeping none to protect the flanks, and one whole half of his phalanx arrived late to the battlefield. At Magnesia, as we shall see, Antiochus' left-wing flank protection routed unexpectedly exposing the phalanx even as he won on the right. At Pydna Perseus apparently did not even commit his cavalry to the battle line and so on the only known occasion a phalanx fought a battle with no flank support at all. On such small chances do the fortunes of empires rest.

Rome was perhaps lucky that it fought generals who failed to utilize their army correctly, or who were foolishly over-reliant on the phalanx alone for victory. This obsession with the phalanx at the expense of other units and ignorance of past tactics cost the Macedonians their kingdom. In addition, this obsession with the phalanx prompted Polybius to see in these three battles an inherent superiority in the Roman formation. The formation alone did not win Rome these battles; poor generalship did in enabling the Roman soldiers to attack the flanks of the phalanx when not protected by other units in a combined arms system.

5. 'Afterwards whether the phalanx drives back by its charge the force opposed to it or is repulsed by this force, its own peculiar formation is broken up.' (18.32)

It is easy to attack gaps that appear in the phalanx's front.

Polybius' criticism here again is that it is easy for the Roman soldiers to go through gaps within the phalanx and engage the phalangites at close quarters. Gaps that appear in the front of the formation are indeed the principal problem of any phalanx. Difficult terrain could cause gaps, but there were ways to counter that. As discussed above under problem 1, Alexander's phalanx at Issus suffered the worst losses of any of his engagements when a gap appeared crossing the river. The Greek hoplites opposite forced their way into the gap and killed many soldiers and officers. It is not clear if the 4,000 Greeks fought their way directly through the phalanx to make their escape or escaped another way. If they did go through the gap, then it was a massive area that no number of reinforcements could have plugged. However, if it was smaller such as might appear between just a few ranks, then the officer could bring rear ranks of the phalanx forward to plug the gap. In the case of Issus the regimental commander, poor old Ptolemy, likely brought forward troops from the rear ranks and died for this crucial effort that saved the battle.

The key question is how the phalanx deployed its rear rank units. I believe that it was possible to leave a gap between the first 8 ranks (8 rows of 8 ranks was the basic unit with a junior officer) and the second 8 (16 rows of 8 ranks was the basic unit with its own officer and adjutants such as messengers and standard-bearer). This gap allowed for the officers, who stood in the rear, to communicate with other units and if needed extend the formation or redeploy.[13]

If this was not the case, then indeed there was no possibility for officers to plug gaps in the phalanx. Therefore, any gaps that did appear would indeed be extremely detrimental to the survival of the phalanx formation. Unfortunately, there is no definitive evidence for the battlefield organization of the phalanx either in the time of Philip II and Alexander or in the later Hellenistic armies. Even the Hellenistic military manuals do not go into the specifics of where officers stood. This has led to a lot of speculation among scholars. However, I favour my own interpretation, delineated in more detail in my prior article, that officers commanded from the rear and that the basic unit deployed in two sections of 8x8. This interpretation provides an option to officers and generals for plugging gaps in the phalanx.

Gaps appearing are something that must have happened repeatedly in Hellenistic battles, yet we never hear about it except at Issus and the battles with the Romans. Certainly, when fighting against other phalanxes the appearance of gaps was not as devastating. However, there are many battles where the phalanx fought units of soldiers armed differently and on rough terrain, most notably Pyrrhus against the Romans in Italy. Yet in none of those do we hear of gaps in the phalanx leading to defeat. It is unlikely that the armies of the early second century simply forgot how to organize phalanxes to prevent or counteract gaps. Phalanxes in some form were in use continually from Philip II through to the Roman annexation of Egypt after Actium. As the generations changed, the phalanx remained and therefore its organization and hierarchy must have also remained almost unchanged. It is much more likely that the Romans took advantage of gaps in the phalanx only in these three crucial battles because of inferior generalship, lack of combined arms, and worse individual experience of the armies they fought.

6. 'For either in following up a retreating foe or in flying before an attacking foe, they leave behind the other parts of their own army, upon which the enemy's reserve have room enough in the space formerly held by the phalanx to attack no longer in front but appearing by a lateral movement on the flank and rear of the phalanx.' (18.32)

The Roman formation has a reserve, whereas the phalanx exposes the rest of the army in advance or retreat and the enemy can attack its vulnerable flanks.

Polybius' argument in this section is valid in terms of how the two formations compare. The great advantage of the Roman formation over almost any other is that it did maintain a reserve of infantry whose officers could reroute reinforcements to wherever required in the battle. The phalanx certainly did not have this possibility if all sixteen ranks fought behind each other. However, I have argued elsewhere that the Macedonian-style phalanx could utilize only eight ranks in the phalanx and have the other eight waiting behind with officers and messengers in between. If this were the case, the rear ranks could move a little to adjust for gaps appearing in the phalanx or turn and face the rear and create a phalanx square.

Without presenting all the prior arguments here again, Alexander the Great's phalanx at Issus saw a large gap appear in the formation because of the impassable nature of the riverbank. Arrian states that more than 120 Macedonians including the regimental commander died trying to fill the gap. With all sixteen ranks of the phalanx fully engaged, there would be no soldiers available to fill that gap. Arrian's account only makes sense if the senior officers brought other ranks of the phalanx from the rear to fill the gap. The only way that could happen is if the phalanx was eight deep, not sixteen. Secondly, Brasidas, the famous Spartan general, utilized a marching square of the phalanx to extricate his hoplites from flat terrain when he had no cavalry support. Other phalanxes also formed defensive squares in battle to escape; see, for example, Magnesia. So, the phalanx formation could function in a square that included reinforcements in the rear. Additionally, the Hellenistic military manuals that discuss the sarissa phalanx provide manoeuvres that the phalanx utilized in practice, one of which was creating a phalanx square or adjusting the frontage of the unit, though admittedly not while actually engaged in combat.

Therefore, the main difference between the flexibility of the Roman and phalanx formations was in the ability to move troops elsewhere while the front ranks were engaged in combat. The phalanx did have a limited ability to commit rearward troops into the phalanx to plug gaps and to become a square, but because of the unwieldy nature of the sarissa troops could not move quickly from one side of the battle to the other. Roman soldiers were able to move completely across the battlefield at will while not compromising the ability to maintain hand-to-hand combat on the front line.

Macedonian-style armies could address the lack of flexible movement of the heavy infantry phalanx. They did so by posting other units of heavy, medium and light infantry as well as heavy, medium and light cavalry and elephants on the flanks of the phalanx. In deploying a fully integrated combined arms army, the battle line extended so far beyond the flanks of the phalanx that it would be quite a march for the Roman infantry to move to attack the vulnerable areas. Moreover, the other units' role in the battle was specifically to protect the flanks of the phalanx whether moving forwards, backwards or remaining stationary.

Therefore Polybius' other criticism is incorrect that the phalanx exposed its flanks whether it advanced or retreated. If it advanced, the other units advanced with it. If it withdrew, so did the others. Both movements should not expose the flanks if the army deployed using combined arms. The only occasion when the phalanx's movement would expose its flanks was if the units next to it routed so much that it exposed the flanks.

The best example of this is Antiochus' victory at Panion as discussed above. The Egyptian phalanx advanced against the Seleucid formation with its flanks protected by a force of Aetolian cavalry. Antiochus' elephants then charged and routed the cavalry, thus exposing the flanks of the Egyptian phalanx as it advanced.

Alexander the Great's battle at Gaugamela best exemplifies the forward movement protection. In that engagement the Macedonian battle line extended more than at any other battle and still did not reach half the Persian line. To prevent exposing the flanks of the phalanx Alexander posted a variety of infantry units, most notably the elite hypaspists and the Agrianian javelin men, whose task was specifically to maintain connection between the phalanx and the cavalry. He also posted a unit of Greek allied hoplites to protect the rear. It was so successful that no gaps appeared in the phalanx and the Persians were not able to attack any parts of the phalanx other than its front.

Antiochus at Panion clearly protected the flanks of his phalanx as it retreated, perhaps deliberately, by using elite heavy infantry, cavalry and elephants. However, perhaps the best example of units shielding the phalanx in retreat is Philip II's victory at Chaeronea. This is the first battle that definitely relied on the sarissa phalanx in battle and the beginning of the use of the tactical withdrawal, a tactic that became standard in Macedonian-style armies. In this case, the phalanx even withdrew up a hill while maintaining formation. Philip protected the flanks of the retreating phalanx on one side with light infantry posted on some foothills and on the other with the assault force of heavy cavalry led by his son, the future Alexander the Great.

As we can see, if the army utilizes and deploys combined arms correctly the flanks of the phalanx are sufficiently well protected whether it moves forward or backward. This, then, nullifies Polybius' criticism about exposing its flanks because of the movement of the phalanx both forward and backward.

7. 'Again, those who employ the phalanx have to march through and encamp in every variety of country; they are compelled to occupy favourable positions in advance, to besiege certain positions and to be besieged in others, and to meet attacks from quarters the least expected.' (18.32)

The final military problem Polybius sees with the phalanx is its ability to carry out normal army practices. The first he lists is marching through every variety of country. Polybius seems to imply that marching with a sarissa over rough country is difficult. Yet his prior arguments about terrain involved the phalanx in battle. In view of the distance and various types of terrain that Alexander covered in his campaign in Asia, there is no evidence anywhere to prove that marching with a sarissa was more difficult than with other weapons.

The soldiers held their sarissa upright when marching and they could easily rest it upon their shoulders. Most scholars accept that it was possible to take the sarissa apart into two halves for ease of transportation. Otherwise, finding wagons to carry 15 or 18ft-long pikes would be very valuable throughout the East. Moreover, Alexander could not have marched his army through forests, over the Hindu Kush and through the mountains of modern Turkey or Afghanistan in inhospitable terrain where tanks still lie abandoned at the side of the road. Nor could Pyrrhus have even conceived of marching his men at night through uncharted woods at Beneventum and expect to remain concealed from the Romans.

In my ongoing efforts in experimental history, I have marched around volunteers holding sarissas and they proved very capable of marching over any ground with the sarissa upright. The difficulties appeared only when trying to cover rising or stony terrain with the sarissa lowered, as it would be in battle. Yet even then, they were able to figure out after only a few attempts how to cross successfully over a small but deep ditch.[14]

So Polybius' criticism of marching is entirely unfounded and not corroborated in any other surviving source over the 300-year existence of the sarissa. As for encamping in rough country, this was one of the normal tasks of any soldier in any army throughout history. In fact, Livy has Hannibal praising Pyrrhus as the second-best general ever in history among other things because 'he was the first who taught how to lay out a camp' (35.14). Pyrrhus' army certainly fought with sarissas yet invented the art of camping properly.

Similar to foraging discussed above, making a camp did not require soldiers to use the sarissa. The soldiers could easily make the necessary fortifications after putting aside their sarissa. Roman soldiers did not build fortifications while carrying their javelins. Nor did the difficulty of the terrain impact the ability to make camp whether armed with a sarissa or not. Polybius is entering into the realm of the absurd by suggesting that the sarissa makes camp-making difficult.

He likely meant that it was difficult to defend the camp quickly if the need arose and this is true. It would take the soldiers a long time to pick up their sarissas and prepare to fight in a formation, time that would likely see the enemy breach the camp. However, that does not mean they did not make camp. There are very few instances throughout ancient warfare of an enemy attacking an army while it was in the middle of pitching its camp. Generals, quite rightly, did not expect to have to fight off the enemy and pitch camp at the same time. If they saw the enemy, they would engage them before making camp, or withdraw and camp elsewhere. The whole point of sending out scouts on horseback was to locate the enemy as well as suitable locations for a camp. Moreover, if Hellenistic soldiers did have to defend a camp, just as in defending a city, they would use their shields and spears, not their sarissas. The traditional hoplite panoply was much more suitable for defending walls or ramparts.

Polybius' next point was that an army had 'to occupy favourable positions in advance', something all armies certainly did. For Macedonian-style armies, the light infantry or the elite heavy infantry unit (hypaspists, peltasts, Argyraspids or others depending on the state) always carried out this task. On many occasions in Hellenistic history from Alexander to Antiochus, generals sent advance forces, but they always sent units separate from the sarissa phalanx. It may have been a detachment of the whole phalanx tasked to act independently, but these troops usually carried spears and shields, not sarissas.

One of the most striking and successful examples is when Alexander the Great sent his hypaspists forward to occupy a hill overlooking his line of attack. In order to get there before the enemy he had his hypaspists ride the horses of his cavalry and dismount on arrival to fight as heavy infantry.[15] Once again, Polybius misunderstood that often the spear replaced the sarissa as the weapon of choice in certain military circumstances. He also failed to discern a difference between the sarissa phalanx as a whole in battle and the individual units of the elite heavy infantry guard. These guard regiments appear in every single Macedonian-style army and one of their primary functions was to act as the advance force of heavy infantry: whether in the phalanx formation or not.

This same argument can similarly counter Polybius' claim that the sarissa prevented attacking and defending fortified positions. There are very many instances of Macedonian-style armies assaulting fortified positions, whether a siege of a city, an attack on a fort or against an enemy dug in on a hillside. These examples abound with both successes and failures as is expected, but in almost every case the attacking soldiers fought with spear and shield, not sarissa. Indeed, as Polybius implied, it would be very difficult, if not impossible, to carry a sarissa up a ladder and over a wall. Such a feat was not required. Soldiers could capture a wall just as well with a spear and shield as with a sarissa. In fact, using the former equipment allowed for protection from missiles and enemy attack when fighting in an individual manner as befitting a siege.

Clearly, neither attacking nor defending forces could form a phalanx on the walls. Yet the walls were the place of prime combat in a siege. Just as in occupying advance terrain, the majority of units that made the initial attacks on city walls were elite heavy infantry supported by missile troops. The phalanx troops usually came in support as the elite unit rarely had sufficient numbers to capture a city on its own. When they did so they also fought with spear and shield.

Alexander the Great's various sieges provide the best evidence for how the sarissa phalanx used different arms. At Halicarnassus, Tyre, Gaza, the Rock of Aornos, against the Malli and so forth, the elite hypaspists first led the attack on the walls followed by the regiments of the sarissa phalanx. I know of no example where soldiers attempted an attack against city walls armed with a sarissa; it was a completely unnecessary and overly-complicated manoeuvre.

There are, however, numerous examples of armies attacking breaches made in city walls armed with sarissas. In such a situation the reach of the sarissa provided benefits over the spear and shield. Fighting over a breach did not normally require the use of a ladder and so both hands were free to hold the sarissa. Moreover, the purpose of an assault on a breach was to create a bridgehead through which to expand out into the streets and gain control of the city. Attacking over the wall instead of through a breach usually resulted in capturing the towers of the wall, and expanding into the city often proved a step too far. A breach in the walls allowed the attackers to thrust more men into the city faster in an effort to overwhelm the defenders.

Often Hellenistic generals sent elephants into a breach to force the enemy back. This usually backfired horribly. The defenders could use the rubble or spikes and projectiles to goad the elephants into turning back onto their own side with dire consequences for the attackers, such as Polyperchon at Megalopolis and Pyrrhus at Argos.

Initially creating a successful bridgehead was easier to accomplish with a sarissa since its length pushed the enemy back faster. However, once the fighting spread out into the streets the sarissa became more of a hindrance than a help since its size prevented soldiers from advancing down narrow or twisty alleys or into houses. Streets were usually wide enough for both defenders and attackers to form their men into a phalanx of spearmen, just as hoplite phalanxes. In close combat in a city, even more than on a battlefield, the frontal defence of a phalanx was difficult to overcome. Since the city walls often made it difficult to expose its flanks the phalanx was safe as long as no other undefended streets led to its rear.

For attackers, once inside the city it was imperative to quickly clear out houses and other buildings along the route. The advantage lay with the defenders in being able to throw missiles onto the attackers, even roof tiles and other household items as projectiles. Such speed of attack into the enclosed alleys or houses of a city was indeed impossible to achieve with a sarissa, just as Polybius states. However, we rarely ever hear of Hellenistic armies even attempting such a thing. Soldiers attacked with spear and shield, whether up a ladder or once through a breach. Once more Polybius fails to realize that Hellenistic armies used the spear instead of the sarissa when the situation demanded it.

However, in defending fortified positions, the greater reach of the sarissa was actually a distinct advantage over a spear, sword or javelin. Philip V's sarissa phalanx successfully defended a breach in the walls at the Roman siege of Atrax. Such was the carnage caused by the sarissas that the Roman soldiers apparently feared ever facing the phalanx again (Livy 32.17-8). Similarly, as discussed in Chapter 4, Antiochus' phalanx proved very successful in defending the wall at Thermopylae when using sarissas from a greater height. Ptolemy I Soter successfully defended the Fort of the Camels against Perdiccas' assault, even using sarissas to blind the attacking elephants and kill their mahouts (Diodorus, 18.34).

For defenders, the prime goal was to prevent attackers from establishing a bridgehead. The best way was to keep them off the walls or the rubble for as long as possible. The sarissa provided the best means to achieve this since its length gave an extra 6ft of range over attackers coming with spear and even more over those armed with a sword. Even defending atop walls, the sarissa could prove effective in stabbing down into the faces of those climbing ladders. If the attackers managed to scale the ladders, the defenders could easily switch sarissas for spears, swords, axes or any other weapon more suited to hand-to-hand combat in the close confines of the ramparts.

As for defending the breach, the sarissas again proved useful in forming a phalanx in the confines of the streets. The phalanx's flanks would be well protected by the walls so that even small detachments of soldiers could successfully hold one narrow passageway provided the houses alongside did not fall to the enemy. Other defenders or citizens would throw missiles onto the attackers while they faced down the hedge of sarissas presented by the phalanx. Defenders did not have to enter houses or other buildings as did attackers, and light infantry, dismounted cavalry or other heavy infantry armed with spears or swords could defend buildings where necessary.

Thus, for defence of fortified positions the sarissa actually proved beneficial over other weapons. For attacking, as in foraging, the soldier of the sarissa phalanx would use a spear and shield instead, something that Polybius completely ignored. This made the phalanx soldiers perfectly capable of carrying out all the necessary military tasks. It would be extremely strange for a military system that proved successful for more than two centuries to be unable to do even basic military activities such as foraging, marching, defending and besieging. However, Polybius did not see it that way.

For his final criticism of this section, Polybius has forgotten, again, that other units existed in Macedonian-style armies besides the phalanx. Yes, the phalanx could not meet attacks from other quarters when deployed in battle with its sarissas lowered, but it was not expected to do so. The heavy infantry without a sarissa, the light infantry and missile troops or the cavalry and elephants had the task of opposing any flanking or rear attacks. This was the whole point of utilizing combined arms tactics. Without these other units and combined arms, the phalanx was extremely vulnerable and inflexible, but that is how it was designed to better serve its primary function in battle: to advance slowly forward, holding secure the centre of the battle line and overcoming every unit in its forward path. Polybius completely ignored this and assumed that Hellenistic armies only comprised a sarissa phalanx and nothing else. This is what happened at Cynoscephalae and Pydna, but that was the fault of the generals, not the phalanx.

8. 'The phalanx soldier can be of service neither in detachments nor singly.' (18.32)

The final criticism Polybius makes is that the Roman soldier can act independently whereas the sarissa-armed soldier must fight in the phalanx. In this he is correct. The sarissa is a terrible weapon for individual or small-scale combat. The famous duel between the Macedonian Coraghus and the naked Greek Dioxippus with his club demonstrates the ineffectiveness of the sarissa one-on-one. However, the Macedonian phalanx soldier equally trained in fighting with spear and shield in the traditional Greek hoplite manner rather than just with the sarissa. A soldier armed with spear and shield could easily function as an independent soldier outside the phalanx formation.

Just as hoplites did not have to fight in a phalanx despite using the heavy 3ft-diameter hoplon shield, Macedonian soldiers armed with the smaller pelte shield could fight well on their own when armed with a spear or sword. The hundreds of examples of spear-armed soldiers fighting in sieges demonstrate the effectiveness of the spear in individual combat. Soldiers trained in these techniques in the Classical Greek world through Pyrrhic dances (a type of war dance), and presumably these traditions continued in the Hellenistic period. Throughout history before the modern age many different cultures chose the spear as the primary weapon of heavy infantry in close combat precisely because of its effectiveness.

So once again, Polybius was wrong because he did not allow for the Macedonian soldiers using different weapons other than the sarissa under any circumstances. He more than anyone else in history was so focused on the sarissa phalanx that he had tunnel vision and did not even acknowledge the other units in a Macedonian-style army, yet these other units were just as important in bringing victory.

Conclusions Concerning Polybius' Comparison

Polybius' comparison is completely flawed. Generals of Macedonian-style armies were not so foolish as a whole to disregard the limitations of the sarissa or of the phalanx. They were very aware of these limitations since their victory in battle depended on mitigating their exploitation while attacking the very same vulnerabilities in the enemy phalanx.

The Roman style of warfare held advantages over a phalanx fighting on its own, but did not benefit from any definitive advantage over a Macedonian-style army that made correct and full use of combined arms. Such an army relied on a phalanx as its core unit, but the success of the whole very much depended on the sum of its constituent parts. Just as Iphicrates argued, each unit in a Macedonian-style army held specific roles as the parts of a body, and if one part failed the whole body was not as effective as it could be. This usually led to its defeat against a more able body that did get the most out of its parts.

There is no obvious tactical or equipment reason why the Roman legionary armed with a javelin and sword fighting in a manipular chequerboard deployment should be inherently superior to the sarissa phalanx in a combined arms army. The sarissa phalanx was a crucial part of the army as a whole, but could never ensure victory on its own. However, the Roman legionary could and did fight successfully without a combined arms army. In my view, the only reason why the phalanx succumbed to the Romans so badly at Cynoscephalae, Pydna, and as we shall see at Magnesia, was because of bad generalship, not inherent comparative inferiority as scholars following Polybius usually argue.

Combined arms were crucial for Macedonian-style armies. Whenever and wherever generals failed to make use of the correct combined arms tactics in deployment and engagement they brought defeat on themselves. Even in just the few battles discussed in this book, Antiochus at Raphia and Scopas at Panion both clearly demonstrate what happened if a general failed to use other units to shield the flanks of the phalanx sufficiently. The lesson was well-known and well-taught through the years, yet fortunately for the Romans the three generals they faced in the second century failed to live up to their ancestors' plentiful examples and paid for it dearly.

Chapter Six

The Naval War with Rome

Antiochus had initiated the war with Rome and failed spectacularly with his efforts. The unmitigated disaster in Greece left Antiochus devoid of 10,000 of perhaps some of his better infantry, six elephants and any chance of taking the initiative. Antiochus moved back to Thrace to join his army that he should have brought into Greece. He likely hoped that Rome would be content to regain control of Greece and leave Antiochus to his domains in Thrace and Asia. Unfortunately for Antiochus, the Romans were determined to press their advantage.

Antiochus fled to Ephesus and according to Livy (36.41), he did not immediately begin preparing for Rome to continue the war into Asia:

> All this time Antiochus was stopping in Ephesus quite unconcerned about the war with Rome as though the Romans had no intention of landing in Asia. This apathy was due either to the blindness or the flattery of most of his councillors. Hannibal, who at that time had great influence with the king, was the only one who told him the truth. He said that so far from feeling any doubt about the Romans going, his only wonder was that they were not there already.

This is perhaps hyperbole from Livy raising Hannibal's reputation and downgrading Antiochus' ability, but from the way Antiochus undertook the war with Rome it does not seem too far-fetched. Antiochus had not thought through his invasion of Greece and he did not fully prepare to face Rome after it failed. Livy states that he focused on naval combat, but he should have ignored the vast expense required to outfit a fleet capable of defeating Rome and its allies. Rather he should have relied on preparing the best army he could to face Rome in battle. Rhodes in particular was a maritime state and prided itself on its excellent navy. Also as Hannibal warns (Livy 36.41, author's emphasis), the Roman navy had become extremely good after constantly fighting the Carthaginian fleets in the Punic Wars:

> The voyage, he pointed out, from Greece to Asia was shorter than from Italy to Greece, and Antiochus was a more dangerous foe than the Aetolians, *nor were the arms of Rome less potent on sea than on land*. Their fleet had been for some time cruising off Malea, and he understood that fresh ships and a fresh commander had come from Italy to take part in the war. He begged Antiochus therefore to give up all hopes of being left in peace. Asia would be the scene of conflict, for Asia itself he would have to fight by sea and by land, and either he must wrest the supreme power from those who were aiming at worldwide dominion or else he must lose his own throne.

Antiochus spent a considerable fortune and time to create a navy to resist Rome and its allies and to prevent an expected Roman crossing to Asia. Unfortunately, he had little hope of ever gaining naval superiority with the forces he had.

Once the Roman fleet arrived in Greek waters, according to Livy (36.43) Antiochus fell back from defending the Hellespont to decide what to do: 'Antiochus abandoned his designs in the Hellespont and returned to Ephesus with all possible speed, taking his warships with him. He at once called a council of war to decide whether he ought to risk an engagement.'

That Antiochus needed to seek advice shows how little confidence he had to take the lead in the war himself. We do not hear from Livy or Polybius of Philip V taking so many war councils in his war on Rome as did Antiochus. In the council Antiochus' admiral, an exiled Rhodian called Polyxenidas, argued for an immediate attack before the allied fleets could join the Roman. This was good advice, but his later arguments that Antiochus' fleet had an advantage are patently false:

> They would not be so very unequally matched in point of numbers and in everything else they would have the advantage, in the speed of their vessels and in various other respects, for the Roman ships were awkwardly built and slow, and as they were going to a hostile country they would be heavily laden with stores, whilst the king's

ships, having none but friends all round them, would carry nothing but soldiers and their equipment.

Clearly Polyxenidas needed to exaggerate to win the argument and gain command, but other officers must have seen the fleets as entirely equal and no navy sails into battle carrying its stores unless ambushed en route. Moreover, Antiochus' fleet of seventy decked ships and thirty smaller ones was weaker in size of ships than even just the Roman contingent. The Roman fleet numbered eighty-one decked ships and other smaller ones, according to Livy (36.42). With the addition of the Pergamene and Rhodian ships, not to mention any that came from Philip V, the Roman allied force would be far too strong for Antiochus. He and his advisors must have known that from the start.

As it was, before Polyxenidas could engage the Romans on their own, Eumenes of Pergamum brought twenty-four decked ships and other smaller ones to join the Roman navy. That gave the Romans a decisive numerical advantage and most importantly a clear superiority in the total of decked battle ships. Livy (36.43) states that 'they put to sea with one hundred and five decked ships and about fifty open ones.'

Unsurprisingly, the Romans easily defeated Antiochus' navy at Corycus. He should have seen that his confidence in Polyxenidas was entirely misplaced and that the Roman fleet was overwhelmingly too large to defeat or even face on equal terms, especially since Antiochus was trying to assemble a fleet from cities in Syria and other regions that he had only recently captured and which did not maintain complete loyalty to him. Antiochus' fleet could not call on a large number of expert sailors or marines or even those who had had much experience in sea battles.

Livy (37.8) states that after this first defeat Antiochus 'devoted himself mainly to fitting out his fleet in order that he might not be deprived of all command of the sea'. His entire strategy of survival relied on preventing a Roman army from crossing into Asia. The leaders were notable in the approaching Roman army. The consul was Lucius Cornelius Scipio and he brought with him his brother, the infamous Publius Cornelius Scipio Africanus, the conqueror of Carthage in the Second Punic War.

Africanus' presence is all the more notable since Antiochus welcomed the advice of Scipio's erstwhile opponent Hannibal. The two foes faced off again as advisors to the main general. Perhaps Livy is correct when later (37.26) he states that Antiochus felt he could not defeat a Roman army commanded by the two Scipios and that this is what spurred on his naval strategy.

Preventing the Romans from crossing the Hellespont required complete naval superiority. Antiochus clearly thought he would be able to gather a navy able to face the Roman fleet and defeat it. Livy continues (37.8): 'The less his success in the past, the greater must be his energy in preparing for the future.' This is a commendable amount of resolve from Antiochus, but the writing was on the wall. He would need a truly massive navy to be able to counteract the fact that the enemy crews were more skilled and experienced than his own.

Though Antiochus' fleet did win one victory against Rhodes on its own at Panormus, thanks to the machinations of Polyxenidas pretending to turn traitor (Livy 37.10-3), it was not enough to force them out of the war completely as should have been Antiochus' intention. Moreover, it came after his earlier defeat against the larger combined navy of Rome and Eumenes of Pergamum. Therefore it is not surprising that Polyxenidas refused to face the combined Roman and Rhodian fleet when they offered battle by blockading Antiochus' navy in Ephesus (Livy 37.13).

Antiochus' navy, even after a winter spent in preparing it, was smaller than the Roman allied fleet in total ships, large ships, and was deficient in the quality of both the sailors and the soldiers. This must have been a huge loss of prestige for Antiochus for his navy to refuse battle on his own doorstep. Yet none of our sources record the consequences of Polyxenidas' refusal to fight. After Antiochus' expedition to Pergamum (see below), Hannibal commanding a section of the Seleucid fleet was soundly beaten by the Rhodian navy at Side (Livy 23-4). This should have confirmed to Antiochus that his fleet and even his best admirals were far too outmatched.

The battle for naval supremacy was a lost cause and would not even be a close contest. Antiochus should have realized this sooner. Instead, he put all his efforts into making the naval confrontation the decisive action to stop Rome invading Asia. The time and resources he should have used to stop Rome from advancing on land he spent in trying to subdue coastal cities and building an even bigger yet untried fleet.

Attack on Pergamum

When Antiochus did attempt to subdue cities in Asia Minor the threat of Eumenes, king of Pergamum, together with the Rhodians proved too much. His main goal was to force the submission of Pergamum, or at least prevent Pergamene aid to Rome. Of all his efforts in this year after Thermopylae this was the most sensible. Removing Pergamum from the war would deprive Rome of enough ships to make any contest at sea more even.

Livy (37.18) states that Antiochus had left his eldest son Seleucus with an army in northern Asia Minor tasked with maintaining his hold on coastal cities in Aeolis near Pergamum. Livy continues that Seleucus crossed to harass Pergamene territory and besieged with a considerable army the port city of Pergamum called Elaea. Without explanation as to why, Livy states that Seleucus abandoned the siege of Elaea and set to ravaging the territory before advancing on Pergamum itself. Since Antiochus met Seleucus there with a large army, it is likely that Antiochus commanded the change in location.

Polybius (21.10) states that Antiochus brought his whole army including a cavalry total of 6000, and Livy (37.18) states he had a vast army including 4,000 Gallic mercenaries (Livy reiterates the 6,000 cavalry number later). Antiochus had finally adopted a strategy that would harm the Roman alliance and greatly increase his hold on Asia Minor by conquering Pergamum itself. Though we have no details of Antiochus' siege, it seems that he did not completely blockade the city since Eumenes, landing at Elaea, was able to lead a body of troops into his capital. If Antiochus' goal was the complete conquest of Pergamum as it should have been, then this was a disastrous turn of events.

Eumenes arrived with reinforcements at Elaea, managed to find his way into Pergamum and refused to fight a battle. Livy (37.18) emphasizes that almost as soon as the Roman fleet arrived at Elaea where he had his camp, Antiochus in fear sued for peace.

Never, it seems, did Antiochus try to besiege Pergamum entirely on a full scale to completely remove that thorn from his Asian side and deny Rome its greatest ally in the upcoming war. His efforts were a halfhearted blockade and ravaging the countryside at best instead of an all-out siege, this despite having a huge army according to both Polybius and Livy. This was the one decision that arguably cost him victory in the war.

It is not clear strategically what Antiochus hoped to achieve by simply raiding Pergamene territory. A few lost cattle and treasures would not hamper Eumenes or Rome and took up vital time and resources that Antiochus could not afford to waste. He completely lacked the urgency expected from someone in a fight for his kingdom and his life. He waltzed around Asia Minor attacking a town here and a city there, but never with a concerted goal or strategy as to how he could stop Rome from coming or prevent allies from joining Rome. Once he learned that Rome was prepared to cross its army over the Hellespont he sued for whatever terms he could get. Antiochus did not demonstrate the necessary urgency in capturing Pergamum once and for all.

Eumenes, the Rhodians and the Roman garrison commander refused Antiochus' offer of peace, preferring to wait until the Roman proconsuls arrived (Livy 37.19). His hopes of peace dashed, Antiochus resumed his ineffectual strategy of trying to capture various cities on the coast of Asia Minor. A well-planned and executed Achaean raid on Seleucus' force ransacking Pergamene territory prompted Seleucus to abandon the excuse of a siege and fall back to Ephesus with Antiochus (Livy 37.20-1).

This was a completely disastrous effort at a cohesive strategy against Pergamum. Antiochus had such a large army that Eumenes refused to attempt a battle, yet Antiochus did not use it to its fullest capabilities. He had the resources to attempt a siege, but not the inclination. The arrival of the Roman fleet threatened Antiochus' rear, but even before it came he had not set up a complete blockade of the city. Antiochus seemed to be perfectly content ravaging enemy territory rather than wholeheartedly committing his resources to the capture of the city. It appears that he expected Eumenes to offer battle and when he refused Antiochus did not know what to do and certainly was not prepared or even intending to besiege the city itself.

Antiochus often failed to capture smaller cities in his time in Asia Minor, so it is likely that he was not at all confident in his ability to capture Pergamum. Perhaps his appearance outside the city was simply to draw Eumenes out to fight. Once Eumenes refused to hazard a battle, Antiochus then hoped his forceful presence would encourage the Romans to make peace. If true, Antiochus misunderstood the determination of the Romans to invade through the Scipios and failed to understand that only the consul had the authority to negotiate a peace.

Overall, Antiochus oversaw a very chaotic expedition that achieved nothing of consequence. He did not detach the Pergamene ships from the Roman fleet. He did not capture any Pergamene cities. He did not defeat any of the Pergamene army or fight any kind of battle. Through a display of force, he did not compel Eumenes or the Romans into concessions or a peace treaty. Even one of those outcomes would have been a success for Antiochus. The ineffectiveness of the campaign makes it unclear as to exactly what Antiochus had hoped to achieve in the first place. Whatever his hopes, they were completely dashed and strategically he was back to where he started.

Naval Confrontation

Eventually, after his failed expedition against Pergamum, Antiochus fell back again on Ephesus where he asked Prusias, king of Bithynia, a territory on the southern coast of the Black Sea, to join him (Livy 37.25). Unfortunately for Antiochus, the Romans sent a letter and an embassy promising Prusias they did not threaten his kingdom and that other princes who had joined them had found their territories enlarged afterwards. It had its desired effect and Prusias denied aid to Antiochus.

Polybius, in the fragments that survive, is critical of Antiochus' inaction and wavering strategy and rightly so. He states that after Prusias refused to assist him Antiochus sought to prevent the Roman army from coming to Asia (21.11): 'Antiochus thus disappointed, proceeded to Ephesus, and calculating that the only way to prevent the enemy's army from crossing and generally avert the war from Asia was to obtain definite command of the sea, determined to give battle by sea and thus decide matters.' Polybius provides the reasoning behind Antiochus' decision to try to gain naval superiority.

Livy (37.26) provides another reason for Antiochus focusing so much on his navy: 'It was the impossibility of offering an effective resistance to the Roman army with the two Scipios in command rather than any naval successes in the past or any well-grounded confidence he felt at the time which made him interest himself in his fleet.'

Yet it is not clear why Antiochus should have such a strong belief that he could not oppose the Roman army successfully even if it was commanded by the two Scipios. That he did so at Magnesia was a last resort, but the size of his army and the effectiveness of both his cavalry and phalanx should have given Antiochus hope in facing Rome as it had done for Pyrrhus, Philip V and later Perseus and Mithridates. Victory in naval combat relied much more on the ability of the sailors than ground combat relied on the ability of the soldiers. In a pitched battle, sheer weight of numbers often overcame smaller but better forces, whereas at sea the better sailors could often bring about great victories despite being numerically outmatched. The Athenian victory at Salamis in the Persian Wars is a prime example. Moreover, in a land battle even a losing army could do significant damage to the enemy forces in terms of manpower. However, in a naval battle the victorious fleet usually remained in possession of the sea and so could repair any damaged vessels and rescue any swimming sailors, thus really minimizing their losses.

Despite having the benefit of fighting in home waters, Antiochus' fleet never did enough permanent damage to the Roman fleet to require it to summon reinforcements. Even one major victory may have been enough to tip the scales in favour of Antiochus, but his fleet kept losing. Any lost or damaged ships the Romans suffered in their victories they could easily repair, whereas Antiochus lost scores of ships and crews that he never got back and had to replace. Therefore, his best hope of matching the Roman superiority in soldiers and sailors was on land, not at sea. Unfortunately he did not see it that way and lost any advantage of time that he should have used to prepare an army to face Rome and blocking the Hellespont crossing or choosing the perfect battle site.

Unsurprisingly, the final naval confrontation at Myonnesus was a complete disaster for Antiochus' hastily-gathered fleet (Livy 37.28-30). Though Antiochus fielded eighty-nine ships to the Roman allied fleet of eighty, according to Livy (37.30) the superiority still remained with the Roman and Rhodian sailors. The Rhodian fire ships alarmed the Seleucid fleet into creating gaps in the line which the better Rhodian sailors took advantage. Antiochus lost forty-two ships in the battle according to Livy, almost half his whole fleet, with very minimal Roman casualties of only a handful of vessels. Finally the penny dropped and Antiochus realized that he had no hope of ever overcoming the Roman allied navy.

The Last Resort

As discussed above, joined by fleets from their allies in Asia Minor, Rhodes and Pergamum, the Romans wrested control of the Aegean from Antiochus, who disastrously lost a final naval battle in Teos Bay and only then resorted to gathering an army to face Rome in battle. Once his navy lost the ability to manoeuvre in the Aegean Antiochus withdrew from Thrace, hastily abandoning his gains around the re-founded city of Lysimacheia which he had argued so hard to keep (Livy 37.31). This was the city he had been determined to hold on to in his initial negotiations with Rome and arguably was the reason he had gone to war with Rome in the first place.

What is worse is that the commander of Lysimacheia had been preparing for a siege and the withdrawal of the Seleucid garrison left all those supplies to the Romans (Livy 37.33). By ceding the city to Scipio, Antiochus also gave up his only strategic advantage of lengthening and disrupting the Roman supply lines. Any delay to the Roman advance bought Antiochus more time to prepare his army for the inevitable final confrontation and his abandonment of Lysimacheia perhaps cost him an extra six months or more.

Livy (37.31) rightly criticizes Antiochus for his decision to abandon Thrace rather than to using it to delay the Roman army's advance. He even suggests, as Polybius has Scipio doing later, that holding up the Romans at Lysimacheia may have prompted the Romans to sue for peace on favourable terms:

> Antiochus was now thoroughly alarmed. Driven from the mastery of the sea, he despaired of being able to defend his distant possessions and, adopting a policy which events subsequently proved to be a mistaken one, he withdrew his garrison from Lysimachia to prevent its being cut off by the Romans. It would not only have been easy to defend Lysimachia against the first attack of the Romans, but the place could have stood a siege through the whole winter and this check would have reduced the besiegers to sore straits for provisions. Meantime there might have been some opportunity for coming to terms and securing peace.

Appian (*Syrian Wars* 6.28) goes even further in his criticism of Antiochus, saying that the gods took away his wits:

But Antiochus, who was generally fickle and light-minded, when he heard of his defeat at Myonnesus was completely panic-stricken, and thought that his evil genius had conspired against him…. Everything unnerved him, and the deity took away his reasoning powers (as is usually the case when misfortunes multiply), so that he abandoned the Chersonesus without cause, even before the enemy came in sight, neither carrying away nor burning the great stores which he had collected there of grain, arms, money and engines, but leaving all these sinews of war in good condition for the enemy.

Appian continues in presenting Antiochus' flight as strategically calamitous because his fear got the better of him:

He paid no attention to the Lysimacheans who, as though after a siege, with lamentations accompanied him in his flight, together with their wives and children. He was intent only upon preventing the enemy from crossing at Abydus, and rested his last hope of success wholly on that. Yet he was so beside himself that he did not even defend the crossing, but hastened to reach the interior in advance of the enemy, not even leaving a guard at the straits.

Antiochus' plans apparently rested entirely on gaining naval supremacy. Once that failed, as he should have known it might, he was at a loss about how to continue. This is hardly the mindset of the confident commander as Antiochus is often depicted. He was so afraid of being cut off in Thrace that he completely abandoned it, even after apparently spending considerable time and money to prepare Lysimacheia for a siege and to oppose the Roman advance there. Though he may well have been cut off by the superior enemy navy, Antiochus would have been better placed and had a better chance of ending the war by stopping the Roman army before it ever set foot in Asia.

Moreover, Antiochus apparently did not have a back-up plan of how and where to face the Romans in Asia. If he did not feel confident in trusting his campaign entirely to defending Thrace, or at the very least defending the crossing of the Hellespont, then he should at the same time have gathered an army in Asia just in case he needed it to give time for his levies from all his eastern territories to arrive. It seems that he did not do so and so was caught unprepared when the Romans crossed the Hellespont so fast since there was no force to slow them down. To achieve both things Antiochus should have left his son Seleucus to defend Lysimacheia while he himself gathered an army in Syria in case Seleucus failed to stop the Romans.

It is obvious why Appian sought to explain Antiochus' hasty and foolhardy retreat as temporary madness from the gods. There is little other explanation as to why Antiochus would completely abandon both the first and second most strategically sensible locations to resist the Roman advance without gaining anything by doing so other than time, which he then wasted.

Polybius (21.13) emphasizes Antiochus' inability to know what to do next:

> Antiochus, who, after his defeat in the naval engagement, remained in Sardis neglecting his opportunities and generally deferring action of any kind, on learning that the enemy had crossed to Asia, was crushed in spirit and, abandoning all hope, decided to send to the Scipios to beg for peace.

Antiochus was very much on the back foot once the Scipios' army arrived in Asia Minor. He hastily tried to make peace with Rome on virtually any terms he could get. He offered to Rome all the concessions they had demanded of him and which he had refused before his foolhardy invasion of Greece. Polybius (21.13), as quoted here, and Livy (37.34-5) both confirm Antiochus' offer of peace as well as the Roman counter proposal:

> He gave up Lampsacus, Smyrna and Alexandria Troas, the towns which were the cause of the war, as well as such other places in Aeolis and Ionia as they chose to take among those which had sided with Rome in the present war. He also engaged to pay half the expenses which their quarrel with him had caused them.

The Romans, now with the upper hand, understandably rejected this offer and countered that Antiochus should give up all his territory on the other side of the Taurus Mountains and pay for the whole cost of the war since he had begun it.

Antiochus had instructed his ambassador to enter into private negotiations with Scipio Africanus to try to obtain his favour in negotiating a treaty. Antiochus had Scipio's son captive and offered this man's release as well as much money and revenue-sharing for his favour. Scipio refused and the answer he gave to Antiochus' envoy as provided by Polybius (21.15-Livy 37.36 and Appian *Syrian Wars* 6.29 record virtually the same speech) reveals both the correct course of action Antiochus should have taken as well as his extreme ineptitude as a general in this war:

> Had he made these proposals while he was still master of Lysimachia and the approach to the Chersonese, he would soon have obtained his terms. Or again, even after retiring from those positions, had he proceeded to the Hellespont with his army, and showing that he would prevent our crossing, had sent to propose the same terms, it would still have been possible for him to obtain them. 'But now,' he said, 'that he has allowed our army to land in Asia, when after letting himself not only be bitted but mounted he comes to us asking for peace on equal terms he naturally fails to get it and is foiled in his hopes.'

Scipio, great commander that he was, correctly noted that strategically it was foolhardy for Antiochus to abandon his recently-gained territory in Thrace. In doing so he had given up the land to Rome without a fight and had also ceded the strategic advantage to Rome of being able to advance to the Hellespont unmolested despite the availability of many choice spots for military engagements. Scipio even goes so far as to state that had Antiochus opposed Rome at his earliest opportunity in Thrace, the Romans would probably have consented to a peace treaty.

This emphasizes just how much of a blunder it was for Antiochus to abandon Thrace without even fighting for it. He had not abandoned Greece when faced with the Roman army, even though he commanded a virtually useless force. So why did he choose to stay in Greece and fight at Thermopylae without a decent army but abandon Thrace when he did have a sizeable force and other strategic advantages? This is the key question. Likely the Aetolians had convinced him to stay in Greece, or he was waiting for an army to cross from Asia. However, to abandon Thrace must have been Antiochus' own strategic decision and it smacks of timidity and despair in the face of his recent naval defeat.

Moreover, Antiochus did not even try to prevent the Roman crossing of the Hellespont or face them there before they could advance inland and gain supplies and soldiers from their allies. Just as the Greek army invaded Troy or Alexander the Great fought his first battle at the Granicus soon after his crossing, it was paramount to engage an army very soon after it landed in Asia lest its strength grew to be unassailable. This tenet of military strategy appears readily in all major wars of all eras. Perhaps the most obvious and most striking for a modern audience were the Normandy landings in the Second World War. Once an army can establish its bridgehead, it is hard to stop an invasion succeeding.

Antiochus had ceded all his strategic advantages to Rome and yet gained absolutely nothing. He had not even used the time gained by retreating from Greece to gather a huge army or to remove Rome's allies from the equation. He had achieved literally nothing and had spent his entire time building wasteful and inadequate fleets and sending out fruitless embassies for peace even after his failed attack on Pergamum and his string of naval defeats.

In Polybius' words, Scipio's advice continues to demonstrate how bad Antiochus' position was at this juncture and how dominant was Rome's after such an easy crossing of the Hellespont:

> He advised him, therefore, to take better counsel in his present situation and look facts in the face. In return for his promise about his son, he would give him a piece of advice equal in value to the favour he offered, and that was to consent to everything and avoid at all cost a battle with the Romans.

Now Antiochus of course could not submit to Scipio's demands, nor could he avoid at all costs a battle with Rome. This is just a case of two enemies taking opposing sides of an argument before finding a compromise. Livy (37.36) rightly states, 'These words did not influence the king in the least, he regarded his chances in war as quite safe', and rightly so. In this case, the Romans had absolutely no incentive to seek peace or a compromise and were set on war. Antiochus' minimal offer of concessions to Rome is similar to the offer to split his empire that Darius III, king of Persia, had made to the victorious Alexander after the Battle of Issus. Then as here, the invading general had absolutely no incentive to accept an offer that he could forcibly take after following up his strategic advantages. Antiochus should have known this before, but finally saw the light after Scipio's comments. Polybius states: 'Antiochus, thinking that no more severe demands than the present could be imposed on him even if he were worsted in a battle, ceased to occupy himself with peace, and began to make every preparation and avail himself of every resource for the struggle.'

Antiochus was right that the Roman demands were too much and would be similar to those after a defeat, but that he did not begin gathering an army until after this negotiation seems so carefree as to be untrue. It seems that he did not begin collecting as large an army as he could until the Romans had already crossed the Hellespont into Asia, gaining troops from Pergamum en route. Antiochus was left floundering by the speed of the Roman advance and had little time to gather many forces to add to those he had commanded in Asia Minor.

Again, without trying to be an armchair general, as soon as he fled Greece and, for whatever reason, decided to abandon Thrace, Antiochus should have followed Hannibal's advice and immediately gathered a huge army for an inevitable confrontation. He had fled after the Battle of Thermopylae in early spring 191 and fought the Battle of Magnesia more than a year later. This was more than enough time to gather a large army from all corners of his empire, but only if he gave the command to do so right away. As it was, he delayed mobilizing for a decisive land battle until Rome invaded his territory and gave him no option but to fight. His vacillating between peace and war once again cost him the necessary time to fully organize and prepare an army capable of defeating Rome.

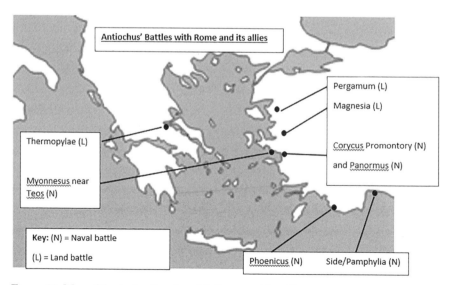

Figure 23. Map of Antiochus' battles with Rome and its allies.

Chapter Seven

The Battle of Magnesia ad Sipylum

On his retreat from Greece Antiochus should have known that the victorious Roman army would soon follow him. Despite desperate attempts to negotiate a treaty, the Romans gave him no choice but to finally accept that he had to select a site for the expected showdown and collect as many troops as he could in the short time he had left. Antiochus knew that his strength was in his phalanx and so needed a flat plain. He also knew that he had to make full use of his cavalry numbers. A wide flat plain would allow his cavalry to expose, hopefully, the flanks and rear of the Roman line.

Macedonian-style armies almost always fought on flat plains wherever they could find them because it enabled the phalanx to maintain its formation more easily. As discussed above, Polybius uses this fact to assume incorrectly that the phalanx could not fight well on uneven terrain, but perhaps more importantly, flat plains allowed the Macedonian-style combined arms army to be able to get the most out of each unit. This was especially the case in allowing the cavalry the space to attack successfully the flanks or rear of the enemy while the phalanx had no trouble holding the centre. Flat terrain was not necessary for a phalanx to function well, but it was ideal ground to provide optimal conditions of success for a combined arms army centred on the phalanx working in concert with significant numbers of heavy cavalry.

The Roman legions rarely succumbed to other armies entirely reliant on infantry. However, as Hannibal proved in the Punic Wars, combined arms armies utilizing expertly-led cavalry forces could gain significant victories. Moreover, since Hannibal Roman armies had not faced an enemy able to command such reserves of excellent heavy cavalry. At Cynoscephalae, as briefly discussed above, Philip V fielded 2,000 cavalry but that force was only equal to if not inferior to the Roman horsemen.

Hannibal proved repeatedly that it was possible to defeat the Roman legion if a general could turn cavalry superiority into surrounding the

Roman forces. Hannibal's successes also came despite commanding heavy infantry forces that were significantly inferior to the Roman legionary. Hannibal showed why he is viewed as such an ingenious tactician by getting his average infantry to survive in the centre of the battle line long enough for the cavalry to surround the Romans and eventually precipitate the rout. Antiochus' phalanx was unmatched in frontal confrontation and certainly very capable of maintaining the centre long enough for the cavalry to surround the enemy. That is the very definition of the hammer-and-anvil tactic that was the mainstay of all successful Macedonian-style armies. Moreover, Antiochus commanded the best heavy cavalry in the world at the time, the cataphracts, as well as almost fifty more elephants than the Romans with which to launch devastating charges into the Roman legions. Antiochus, advised by Hannibal, had the army, units and opportunity to inflict another Cannae on the Romans.

The litany of victories in Seleucid and Hellenistic history prove how important cavalry was, both in protecting the phalanx and exposing the wings and rear of the enemy forces. These are the tactics that had proven successful for almost every Macedonian-style army since Philip II. Yet, not to labour the point, these were the precise tactics Antiochus could not implement in Greece because he had so little cavalry and as a result his army was completely routed at Thermopylae. This was the same error made by both Philip V at Cynoscephalae and Perseus at Pydna later.

Pyrrhus had demonstrated how this tactic could work against the Romans at Heraclea, though he used elephants rather than cavalry as the hammer. Moreover Hannibal, the scourge of Rome in the Second Punic War, was one of Antiochus' advisors. Clearly, Antiochus did not simply take everything Hannibal said as gospel since he had ignored the excellent advice to invade Greece earlier and bring more troops with him, but through Hannibal Antiochus should have known how to ensure that his cavalry would expose the Roman army. Thus, Antiochus had no reason to believe that he would not win the final showdown with Rome provided that on this occasion he organized and utilized his army correctly.

Moreover, Antiochus was the first Hellenistic general to field a force of cataphracts. A unit of very heavy cavalry from Bactria and the east that saw man and horse fully armoured from head to toe, these were the forerunners of medieval knights and their charge was a devastating event, as the Romans discovered against both Mithridates of Pontus and the

Parthians, most famously at Crassus' defeat at Carrhae. This unit clearly demonstrated its effectiveness at the Battle of Panion in easily routing the cavalry opposite them (Polybius 16.18.6-8). This was perhaps the key unit Antiochus called up to his army.

Despite these advantages and strengths, it seems that Antiochus lacked any confidence whatsoever. Livy states more than once that Antiochus did not think he could defeat a Roman army led by Scipio. Perhaps Antiochus really did fear Scipio and that fear was what drove him to try to win the naval confrontation rather than prepare for a land campaign. Whatever the reason, it displayed a complete lack of confidence in his own army and generalship and perhaps explains why the final battle at Magnesia went so badly.

Cavalry was certainly Antiochus' best means of defeating the Romans. As discussed above, the Aetolians leveraged Antiochus' cavalry forces as the means to support him in a war against Rome. '[E]ven if the armies of the whole of Europe were brought together, they would be crushed by these cavalry forces' (Livy 35.48). Yet it is important to note again, when Antiochus landed in Greece to make war on Rome, he brought with him 10,000 infantry but only 500 cavalry (Livy 35.43.6). Antiochus hoped that his arrival in Greece would prompt the numerous local states to join him and enlarge his army. He purposely brought only a minimum force.

He rightly adjudged the need for his expert phalanx in any future confrontation and so brought 10,000 of these troops, but he neglected to bring the required force of cavalry that he would also need. The two must always work in tandem to achieve any success in Macedonian-style warfare. He must have intended the Greek allies to furnish his necessary cavalry forces. Yet the Greeks, except for the Thessalians and the Achaeans under Philopoemen, were not renowned for their cavalry prowess. So his decision to rely on Greek levies of cavalry was extremely negligent. Perhaps it was the Aetolian capture of Demetrias in Thessaly that persuaded him that he now would have access to Thessalian cavalry such as had served Alexander the Great so well. Unfortunately, the hope was unproven and Thessaly as a whole never joined the alliance against Rome.

At Magnesia Antiochus was able to call on large numbers of cavalry of all types. However, he had demonstrated that his command of cavalry in his army verged on reckless. He had snatched defeat from the jaws of victory in his battle with Ptolemy IV at Raphia by wasting his cavalry superiority and initial successes. He did not return with his victorious cavalry to threaten the vulnerable flanks and rear of the huge Ptolemaic phalanx and Ptolemy was able to personally inspire the Egyptian phalanx to victory.[1] At Panion Antiochus had routed the Egyptian army because he successfully used his cavalry and elephants to expose the flanks of the enemy phalanx. However, the quick retreat of the Egyptian cavalry precipitated that victory and it was Antiochus' son who had correctly brought back the victorious right-wing cavalry to threaten the rear while the king remained on the left flank.

Even with cavalry superiority, as Antiochus clearly had at Magnesia, it still required the general to have the ability to make the most of that advantage. Unfortunately, Antiochus proved at Magnesia that he was not a good enough commander to use his advantages to bring victory.

The Battle Lines are Drawn

Livy and Appian state that Antiochus first awaited the Romans at Thyatira, an important city in Lydia situated on a wide plain good for cavalry. Scipio Africanus had been ill and Antiochus returned his son to him, which according to Livy hastened his recovery (Livy 37.37). What is most interesting about this episode is that both Livy and Appian (*Syrian Wars* 6.30) have Scipio, as a sign of his gratitude, advise Antiochus not to attack the Roman army until Scipio himself was there to command it.

This was hardly a beneficial offer. It would certainly have been better for Antiochus to attack the Romans before Scipio was well enough to lead the army. Moreover, as discussed above, it would also have been better if Antiochus attacked before Eumenes of Pergamum had supplied and reinforced the Roman army. However, Livy emphasizes that 'Antiochus was swayed by the authority of the man on whom, in view of the doubtful issue of the war, he had rested all his hopes of support, whatever might betide him.' Appian confirms that Antiochus withdrew to Magnesia ad Sipylum because he was acting on the advice of Scipio and decided to wait. This withdrawal happened despite the size of Antiochus' army and the perfect battlefield location of the plain outside Thyatira.

It seems, according to Appian, that Antiochus' main reason in moving to Magnesia was because it was a defensible position on the side of Mount Sipylus 'with the river Phrygius between himself and the enemy, so that he should not be compelled to fight against his will'. Livy (37.37) states that Antiochus spent his time fortifying his new position:

> He surrounded his camp with a fosse six cubits deep and twelve wide, and outside the fosse he threw up a double rampart, on the inner edge he constructed a wall flanked at short intervals with turrets, from which the enemy could be easily prevented from crossing the fosse.

He must have felt safer with the extra time to prepare a defensive camp at Magnesia rather than risking battle straight away at Thyatira. Yet even at Magnesia, Antiochus did fight the Romans in battle on the plain between the mountain and the river. Tactically, Antiochus' advantage lay in getting the most out of his cavalry as discussed above, and a siege in a fortified camp would completely nullify this. The camp was a literal bulwark of safety in case things went awry in the battle, but Antiochus would have done better to convince his men and his own mind that only a victory in the battle would save them. Julius Caesar at Dyrrachium and many other military commanders throughout history demonstrated how much better an army fights when it knows its only hope of survival lay in victory despite the odds.

Antiochus should have wagered everything on seeking the decisive battle on the plain at Thyatira where his cavalry had the space to surround the Roman army. This is exactly what Scipio expected, betraying what was Antiochus' most logical option. By pulling back to a position of greater safety Antiochus nullified his main advantage in cavalry numbers and thus any advantage he may have had in the decisive battle.

All Antiochus' actions once he finally gave up the naval war betray his lack of confidence in his ability to defeat the Romans or Scipio in battle. Perhaps, as Livy suggests, it really was the presence and reputation of Scipio Africanus that cowed Antiochus into such timid and negative actions in the war. It seems that Antiochus did not know how best to defeat the Romans, nor did he have the confidence that he would, despite the numerical and mobility advantages of his army, and yet Antiochus could still call on Hannibal for advice on these exact topics. Perhaps

Antiochus did not trust in his ability after his naval defeat, or his other counsellors undermined Hannibal. Whatever the reason, Antiochus betrayed the strategy of a general already accepting his defeat.

The early military engagements at Magnesia demonstrate Antiochus' lack of confidence in winning the battle. Livy records (37.38) that more than 1,000 cavalry charged over the river to attack the Roman advance posts, but unsurprisingly this force fell back once the rest of the Roman army arrived on the scene. Other than probing the Roman camp, it is not clear exactly what Antiochus hoped to achieve with this attack. He certainly did not intend to cross his whole army over the river to attack the Romans and there was no way such a small force could cause lasting damage to the Roman army. It was a waste of valuable cavalry in a pointless probing of the enemy position.

Following that initial pointless skirmish, according to Livy the two sides remained on opposite sides of the river for two days before the Romans crossed. As they were making their camp Antiochus sent a 3,000-strong force of picked infantry and cavalry to attack, but the Roman advance guard repulsed them without having to call for aid from those making the camp. Again, without following up this attack with the whole army Antiochus' force could never have done that much damage to the Roman army; it was simply a waste of some of his better troops.

Antiochus delayed another five days and repeatedly declined battle after the Romans moved into the middle of the plain. So surprising was Antiochus' inaction that Scipio held a war council on whether to head into winter quarters if they could not force a battle (Livy 37.39). The Romans preferred to attack the fortified camp and made preparations to do so. Appian (*Syrian Wars* 6.30) has the Roman commander Domitius announce to Antiochus' army that the Romans would attack on the next day whether Antiochus came out to fight or not. Eventually Antiochus decided he could delay no longer lest he dishearten his own men and further embolden the Romans (Appian, *Syrian Wars* 6.30):

> The latter [Antiochus] was perplexed and again changed his mind. Although he would have ventured heretofore only to make a stand under the wall or to repel the enemy from the wall, till Scipio should regain his health, he now thought that with superior numbers it would be disgraceful to decline an engagement. So he prepared for battle.

Once again this betrays Antiochus' fear of Scipio and his lack of confidence in his own abilities. Rather than confirming his position of waiting until Scipio was healthy, this pointless delay in fighting once and for all confirms the general timidity of Antiochus in fearing battle rather than seeking it. Hannibal had repeatedly demonstrated in the Second Punic War that the way to defeat the Romans was to catch them unawares in full force, not by letting them march and molesting them with small detachments.

Had Antiochus adopted an offensive mindset, he may well have caught the Romans unprepared. Moreover, if he had stayed at Thyatira he could have fought them when they were tired immediately after they had force-marched for five days straight. As it was, he delayed and delayed until any further delay would have confirmed his cowardice and he finally rolled the dice and went out for battle. Even then, he did not advance his lines too far from his fortified camp just in case things went wrong. Caution can be a good trait in a commander, but in this case Antiochus was too cautious and it proved detrimental to the morale of his army and a boon to the Romans.

Roman Battle Lines

The Romans had four legions of 5,000 infantry, 3,000 cavalry and 16 elephants (Livy 37.39). The Roman left wing rested on the river secured with 4 squadrons of cavalry, around 120 men. The legions formed up in the centre in the usual fashion. The velite light troops made up the front lines, behind them came the medium infantry hastati, behind them the heavy javelin-armed infantry the principes, and the veteran triarii spearmen brought up the rear. Roman legions drew up in a chequerboard formation to provide flexibility of defence and attack.[2] The Romans placed their sixteen North African elephants behind their infantry since this force was no match for Antiochus' fifty-four Indian elephants, which were bigger animals. The Romans concentrated around 3,000 cavalry on the right wing led by Eumenes of Pergamum's 800 troops. A 3,000-strong force of allied Achaean and Pergamene light infantry Caetrati linked the Roman legions to this cavalry force. Trallian and Cretan missile cavalry rode at the furthest point of the right wing, allowing them the space to manoeuvre and fire their missiles while protecting the right flank. Some

2,000 Macedonian and Thracian volunteers guarded the Roman camp a few miles to the rear. Presumably most of these troops were light infantry peltasts since this was the unit most associated with these two regions.

The Roman battle formation was the standard deployment of most combined arms armies in the ancient world with cavalry on the wings supporting the centre force of heavy infantry. The light and medium infantry linked the cavalry and the heavy infantry. The horse-archers and more mobile light cavalry always fought on the very extremities of a formation where they had the space to manoeuvre at speed and stay away from close-quarter combat.

Antiochus' Battle Lines

Livy states in a rather confused description that next to the phalanx on the right wing Antiochus stationed the following:

1,500 heavy Gallic infantry
3,000 cataphract cavalry
1,000 Royal companion heavy cavalry of the Agema
3,000 Argyraspids heavy infantry peltasts
1,200 horse-archers
3,000 light infantry
2,500 archers
A force of slingers and archers
Finally, 16 elephants as the flank guard

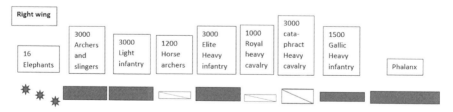

Figure 24. Battle of Magnesia ad Sipylum: Right wing, Livy's deployment description.

Keeping archers and slingers on the flank is understandable as a flank guard able to fire their missiles in on the enemy flank, but this organization separates the heavy infantry into two sections split by the 4,000-strong heavy cavalry force intended to charge the enemy line. When the heavy cavalry charged, it would leave a huge hole in the formation between the slower-moving heavy infantry. This is an entirely original deployment if true.

In my view it is more likely that Livy has confused his source account and that the 3,000 Argyraspids actually stood next to the Gallic infantry, thus maintaining the integrity of the battle line and keeping all the heavy infantry together in the centre. Livy confused unit placements and actions. The mass of light infantry possibly stood in front of the Argyraspids and other heavy infantry, and perhaps also the cavalry, with the horse-archers occupying the far right flank of the army able to wheel around and fire their arrows.

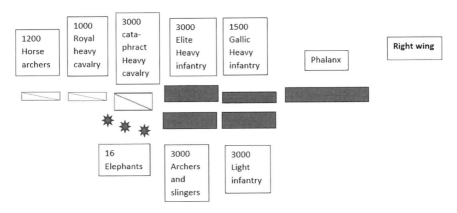

Figure 25. Battle of Magnesia ad Sipylum: Right-wing probable deployment.

Livy's description of Antiochus' left wing is just as confusing and jumbled. He states that next to the phalanx stood the following:

1,500 Gallic heavy infantry
2,000 Cappadocian heavy infantry
A miscellaneous group of 2,700 presumably heavy infantry, though Livy does not describe the nature of this force
3,000 cataphract cavalry
1,000 Royal companion cavalry
Tarantine cavalry
2,500 Gallic cavalry
1,000 Cretans, presumably infantry archers
1,500 Carians and Cilicians armed the same way

1,500 Trallians
4,000 Caetrati peltasts
A force of slingers and archers to match the right wing
Finally, 16 elephants as the flank guard

In front of the heavy cavalry were the camel-archers and in front of them the scythed chariots.

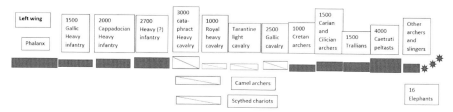

Figure 26. Battle of Magnesia ad Sipylum: Left-wing, Livy's deployment description.

What is most interesting is the deployment chosen by Antiochus for his light infantry. Livy states, if we can believe his account, that Antiochus mixed his cavalry and light infantry in different places in his line as well as providing a screen of light infantry all along the army's front, which was standard and was what the Romans had done. Appian's summary of Antiochus' formation (*Syrian Wars* 7.32-3) is confused and not as specific as Livy's. He assumes the standard deployment of cavalry on either side of the heavy phalanx in the centre, but he then states that a mass of light infantry stood all along the front of the line and that Antiochus' army looked like two armies, one in front and one behind in reserve. Both sources agree that Antiochus placed his camel-archers and scythed chariots in front of the main battle line, but only Livy states that they fought directly before his heavy cavalry on his left wing.

On this wing, at least all the heavy infantry drew up together as expected and that must have been the case on the other wing as well. Once again, it does not make sense for such a strong force of missile infantry to stand to the side or the front of the cavalry and they must have been in front of the heavy infantry as a screen. Appian confirms this if we believe his statement (*Syrian Wars* 7.33) that the Seleucid army looked like two lines, one in the front and one in reserve.

The light infantry peltasts, who could throw missiles and fight in hand-to-hand combat, normally stood as a flexible link in the main line between the heavy infantry and the cavalry. Alexander the Great perfected this system and every Hellenistic general used it in battle. Antiochus probably did likewise, as he did in every other battle, and Livy simply misplaces them in the screen, but it is possible that Antiochus chose a deployment that mirrored the Roman light infantry placement along the front of the whole line.

That Antiochus placed significant numbers of light infantry in front of his cavalry forces is surprising. The problem with this deployment is that the light infantry in front prevented Antiochus' cavalry from having clear sight of the enemy movements or a clear line of attack to charge them. Antiochus' great strength was his heavy cavalry led by the heavily-armoured cataphracts. He should have done everything in his power to engineer an opportunity to launch this devastating cavalry force against the Roman flank, just as Alexander did with his expert Macedonian cavalry at Gaugamela against the Persians. Blocking their front with a mass of light infantry makes little tactical sense.

It is difficult to understand the intended tactics here since the actual battle went so badly for Antiochus right from the start, but he and his advisors must have had some reason for this unusual deployment. The most likely explanation is that he wanted his missile infantry to engage the Roman missile troops before he launched his heavy cavalry charge that would bring his victory. He wanted to oppose the Roman front lines of light velites with his own light troops. If this were the case it is surprising that Antiochus' first action was to send out his scythed chariots rather than engage in a missile duel.

Stationing light troops in front of the whole line was a flawed idea but understandable. However, the deployment of light infantry among the cavalry on the flanks was extremely strange. Such a formation detrimentally reduced the impact and battlefield purpose of the heavy cavalry to charge into the enemy lines.

In my view, taking into account both Appian's and Livy's descriptions and utilizing standard Hellenistic practices, Antiochus' unit deployment probably looked like this:

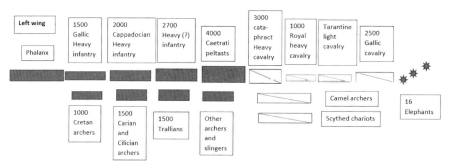

Figure 27. Battle of Magnesia ad Sipylum: Left-wing probable deployment.

So, in summary, Antiochus' battle line likely did follow the traditional combined arms deployment. The heavy infantry sarissa phalanx held the centre, flanked on each side by units of other heavy infantry armed in different fashions. The heavy cavalry stood next to the heavy infantry and the light and missile cavalry protected the flanks. In front of the heavy infantry was a large screen of light and missile infantry and in front of the heavy cavalry on the left wing stood camel-archers and scythed chariots. This must be what Livy describes; he just confuses exactly where the thousands of light infantry units stood in the line.

Elephant(s) and Castle(s)

The other notable deployment in Antiochus' army at Magnesia is the rest of his elephants. At all Antiochus' previous battles and in all Hellenistic battles, the elephants fought on the flanks of the army where they excelled as a static flank guard firing missiles but could be called on to charge the enemy if necessary, just as Pyrrhus had done against the Romans and as Antiochus did at Panion. Antiochus at Magnesia enjoyed such a large advantage in elephants that the Romans did not even deploy theirs to fight in the battle line. Antiochus thus had an advantage in that he could place the elephants wherever they would be most effective rather than having to oppose the Roman animals. Similar to his options at Panion, he could for once use elephants offensively as well as defensively. He followed the standard pattern and placed sixteen elephants on each wing as flank guards. Each force equalled the Roman elephant total and thus would be able to resist any Roman elephant counterattack. This left Antiochus with twenty-two elephants to deploy wherever he wanted to maximize their abilities.

Both Livy and Appian state very clearly that Antiochus chose to place the remaining elephants accompanied by light infantry in between the units of his sarissa phalanx. Two elephants stood between ten divisions of the phalanx drawn up thirty-two ranks deep, leaving two elephants on either side of the whole formation. Both historians describe the line as having the appearance of castle towers within the ramparts of the phalanx.

Figure 28. Phalanx regiments with elephants between.

It is likely this formation was a response of Antiochus to the Roman victory at Cynoscephalae when the legionaries exploited gaps in the phalanx, but this was an unnecessary innovation. As argued above, the phalanx fighting on level ground remained impenetrable to the Roman legions and the Roman major victories occurred where rough terrain created gaps for the legionaries to exploit.

Tactically it would make more sense if the elephants stood directly in front of the phalanx mixed in with the line of light infantry. Light infantry often fight next to elephants since their manoeuvrability allows them to avoid the animals while still pressuring the enemy. Just as the peltasts added strength to the missile troop screen on the flanks, so elephants would add a great strength to any missile screen in front of the phalanx. Pyrrhus had also shown the effectiveness of an elephant charge against the Roman infantry. Antiochus could have had the elephants charge the Roman lines as a disruption to their formation following the missile attack or as a combination with it. The phalanx in its deep formation could then follow up the disorder to press home the advantage on the Romans. The elephants were likely spaced out in twos so that they could withdraw through the phalanx if needed when the phalanx advanced just as the light infantry screen would. From the point of view of the Roman army, whose accounts surely form the basis for Livy and Appian, the elephants would appear to be standing alongside the phalanx rather than just in front of it.

Or:

Figure 29. Phalanx regiments with elephants in front.

However, this is all just theoretical speculation. In the actual battle, the phalanx never advanced to close with the Roman legions, nor did the elephants have time to charge the Roman lines and nor did the light troops have a long missile duel. The carnage on the Seleucid left wing happened so fast that the centre of the battle line had probably not even moved forward. Instead, in order to try to survive the Roman assault, the phalanx formed a defensive square likely punctuated by the elephants. We do not know anything about Antiochus' original intentions for this placement of elephants; whether it was offensive to have the elephants charge or defensive to have them shield the flanks of the phalanx.

Perhaps the elephant location provided in detail in both sources describes how the phalanx appeared to the Romans after it re-formed into a defensive square. It was only at that point in the battle that the Roman army advanced close enough to see the phalanx clearly. According to Livy, the morning haze followed by, in British terms, 'mizzle' prevented one wing of Antiochus' army from seeing the other and likely prevented each side seeing the other clearly. A defensive square punctuated by elephants at specific intervals would very much appear like a castle with towers at its corners, perhaps more so than the phalanx in a straight line.

Nonetheless, the elephant positioning between the phalanx battalions does make sense as a deterrent to the Roman legions on attacking the flanks. The greater depth of thirty-two ranks suggests that Antiochus intended the phalanx to push its way right through the legions and thus would need extra protection on its sides. Inevitably, not every section of the phalanx would push back the Romans at the same speed and gaps would certainly occur. The presence of the elephants, the only other unit in Antiochus' army that possessed a similar forward offensive firepower to the phalanx, would protect the gaps and cause their own problems for the Romans when charging forward.

An interesting statement from Livy (37.42) may help shed light on the elephants' position in the centre. He states that the Romans knew how to deal with charging elephants because of their experiences in the Punic Wars. They ran around the animals, avoiding their stomping, and attacked the sides with javelins or hamstrung the legs with swords. For the Romans to be able to run around the elephants suggests that the animals were not fighting directly alongside the phalanx. If the Romans had space to run around the elephants, they also had space to run around and between the phalanx battalions and attack the exposed flanks and rear. That is exactly what Antiochus did not want and exactly why the elephants were there if placed between the phalanxes. The battle had turned into a melee, and by that point the defensive square of the phalanx would not work if there were any gaps at all. This description of Roman actions against the elephants strongly suggests that the animals fought in front of the phalanx mixed in with the mass of missile troops and the phalanx came behind.

All of this is, of course, speculation. Since everything went so wrong for Antiochus it is difficult to determine what his tactics were. He certainly intended to launch cavalry charges with cataphracts on each wing, on the left preceded by a chariot attack. In view of the speed with which these units advanced, it is therefore also likely that he intended his phalanx and elephants in the centre to attack and follow up in the centre the gains he hoped to make on the flanks. If all went according to plan, Antiochus' cavalry on the wings could then turn onto the Roman legions in the centre and truly make use of the hammer-and-anvil tactics to drive the legionaries onto the points of the phalanx's sarissas and the feet of the elephants.

If this was the case, then the phalanx would not have to move far in the centre to achieve its purpose in the overall battle plan. Even a static phalanx covered by a screen of missile troops and elephants would function perfectly well as the central anvil for the two cavalry hammers on the wings. Moreover, the large screen of missile troops, perhaps including elephants, would doubly serve this goal by keeping the Roman infantry at bay and at a distance long enough for the Seleucid cavalry to turn both flanks. Had the phalanx advanced too early it may have gone too far, lost its cohesion and allowed the Roman legionaries to hack their way through, as they did at Cynoscephalae.

The Battle

Livy states (37.41) that to begin the battle Antiochus launched his expected attacks on each wing. He led the heavy cavalry charge against the small Roman cavalry force on the Seleucid right wing while his chariots set off as the first wave of his planned cavalry assault on the left wing. Most importantly, what we do not hear from Livy is that at the same time the phalanx started moving forward. Perhaps it did, but the disastrous events on the left wing transpired so fast it meant that the phalanx was little distant from its starting-point.

Antiochus began the battle with the charge of his scythed chariots. Eumenes, having fought Seleucid armies all his life, knew the weakness of chariots and sent his missile troops to attack the exposed horses at a distance. According to Livy, the thousands of missiles did the damage, stopping the chariot attack in its tracks as horses, chariots and men fell about each other in absolute carnage. This in turn routed the force of camel-archers following closely behind. The survivors turned and fled back through Antiochus' own lines as the fastest way to safety.

Eumenes followed up his advantage and launched a cavalry charge straight at Antiochus' cataphracts, which were now exposed and still stationary. The strength of cataphracts is to charge, and standing still they were no match for Eumenes' cavalry charge. The cavalry fled as fast as they could back to the camp. The screen of missile troops very quickly also fled along with the heavier infantry units that linked with the phalanx. Many of these soldiers fled into the phalanx for protection. This wing was a complete disaster for Antiochus and is what led to his defeat.

Livy makes no mention of the sixteen elephants on this wing, but presumably they also fled with little chance to stop the rout themselves. This omission in narrative suggests that the elephants as a flank guard stood on the left flank far out to the side of the cavalry rather than to the side of the infantry with the cavalry behind as would be the usual deployment. Had they been next to the infantry, surely Livy would have mentioned the carnage caused by the elephants retreating through the formations of Seleucid soldiers. If they were far out beyond the cavalry they would simply fall back to the camp without doing any damage to anyone, friend or foe. This placement rather nullifies their advantages for

Antiochus in the battle. So far on the flank the elephants could neither protect the infantry's flank nor charge into the Roman infantry.

On the other wing, Antiochus led a heavy cavalry charge against the four squadrons of Roman cavalry by the river. He burst through easily and turned the flank of the Roman infantry, forcing many of them to flee to their camp. Antiochus, supported by the infantry on the wing, pressed the advantage and chased the Romans back to their camp. The 2,000 men of the Roman camp guard came out and rallied the fleeing soldiers to turn and face Antiochus' victorious cavalry. At the same time Eumenes' brother charged into Antiochus' forces with 200 cavalry sent from the other wing. Now faced with resistance in front and to the side and hearing of the disaster to the rest of the army, Antiochus turned and fled.

The phalanx in the centre, shorn of its cavalry flank protection and unable to get away, formed a defensive square, likely including the central elephants. Many of the light infantry fled inside the square and tried to fight to safety. Eventually the mass of the Roman infantry came to bear on the phalanx and it collapsed into panic-stricken flight back to the camp. The Seleucid camp guards briefly held up the Roman assault, but eventually they also fled and the Romans swarmed the camp, elated in victory.

Chapter Eight

Antiochus' Failure of Combined Arms

It was an unmitigated disaster for Antiochus from start to finish and all because he began the battle on his left wing with a charge of scythed chariots rather than with his cataphracts.

Antiochus' army contained soldiers drawn from all over the Seleucid Empire. To Livy this made the army less reliable since all the units fought in different ways (Livy 37.40), whereas the Roman army fought with uniform armaments, especially the heavy infantry. However, the different fighting styles merely required greater integration and a sophisticated utilization of combined arms.

Alexander the Great and many Hellenistic generals showed the strengths of an army utilizing different types of soldiers. As argued above, regardless of armament, the types of unit all performed the same roles in battle. Antiochus could therefore trust that all his heavy infantry of whatever type would fight well in a melee. He knew his heavy cavalry was best in charging the enemy. He knew his missile troops functioned best in a supporting role skirmishing on the edges or before the melee began. He knew his elephants worked well as static flank guards that could charge effectively if needed and not impeded by other elephants. In fielding every type of unit available including less common ones such as camel-archers and scythed chariots, the problem for Antiochus was how to get the best out of each unit while also protecting against their weaknesses.

Chariots were best used on a retreating enemy safe from a large barrage of missiles where the scythed wheels could cut down horses and men running away. Heavy cavalry, especially cataphracts, were only effective when charging into battle, not standing still receiving a charge. Any cavalry charge on the wings was only successful when the commander turned to attack the exposed flanks of the enemy's centre. Elephants were best saved to charge when the enemy was already on the point of flight, thus minimizing the possibility of being goaded to turn on their own lines and maximizing the likelihood of terrifying the enemy into fleeing. The phalanx did not need to march forward as long as its flanks were secure and needed only to remain in the centre to act as the spiked rampart on which to drive the enemy line. Light infantry should fill in the gaps among other units and only attack before and after the melee. Light cavalry should fight on the flanks harassing as much as possible and then only charge forward when the enemy retreated. Antiochus should have known that camels were slow and the animals vulnerable, though he had no prior experience with such a unit. Likewise, he should have known that chariots were especially vulnerable to light infantry missiles targeting the horses. Eumenes certainly knew this and thus won the battle for the Romans, yet Antiochus did not adjust his battle plan accordingly.

Antiochus' army was well constructed to defeat the Romans. He had enough cavalry to overwhelm the Roman flanks and rear, he had enough elephants to threaten to charge the Roman lines, and he had a strong phalanx in the centre to keep the Romans occupied but at a distance lest the Roman swords cut swathes through the Seleucid infantry. He also had enough missile troops to outgun the Roman velites and enough light cavalry and chariots to pursue the Romans when they fled and turn a defeat into a rout.

Contrary to the common arguments of Roman historians, there was nothing about Antiochus' army that put him at a disadvantage. However, he had to fight the battle correctly to maximize his own strengths and minimize his weaknesses. This is the very foundation principle of combined arms warfare. Unfortunately, he made two costly errors that right from the start caused him to lose the battle. He began on the left with a charge of chariots headlong into a morass of missile troops and he personally failed to lead his victorious cavalry units on the right to attack the exposed Roman flank.

It was the intervention on the Roman side of the Attalid cavalry under Eumenes of Pergamum that really decided the battle. In the battle, Eumenes first used missile troops to nullify the chariots and camels by targeting the animals in a barrage of arrows, sling stones and javelins. Then, though severely outnumbered, in the disordered flight of scores of chariots and incensed horses Eumenes charged his heavy cavalry to rout the entire left wing of Antiochus down to the phalanx, including 3,000 cataphracts. This attack reveals the frightening ability of a veteran heavy cavalry charge even against overwhelming odds[1] and the lack of experience of Antiochus' vast numbers of cavalry. It was this single surprising success of Eumenes that won the battle, and arguably an eastern empire, for the Romans.[2]

On the other flank Antiochus himself led a similarly effective heavy cavalry charge to rout the Roman left wing that rested on the river and was poorly supported by cavalry. The Roman camp guard of 2,000 rallied the retreating men and Eumenes' brother led 200 cavalry around from the other wing, the sight of which prompted Antiochus to flee and the rout spread to the whole army (Livy 37.41-43).

The contrasting successes of the heavy cavalry charge on each wing decided the battle. Had Antiochus' brother, commanding the Seleucid left wing, first charged at Eumenes' numerically inferior cavalry with 3,000 cataphracts and other cavalry instead of the vulnerable camels and chariots, both flanks of the Roman army may have been turned by an overwhelming heavy cavalry charge. At the very least, they may have gained enough parity for Antiochus on the other wing to outflank the Romans and drive them onto the rampart of sarissas and elephants in the centre.

The final event that turned a setback into an unmitigated disaster was Antiochus' own flight. The Roman counterattack caught him off guard after pursuing the routing enemy wing too far, as he had done at Raphia before, and as many other cavalry commanders have done throughout history. Antiochus should have trusted in having turned the Roman flank and charged into the Roman centre rather than pursuing the fleeing troops back to their camp. Even after the chase to the fortified camp, Antiochus could have resisted the rallied Romans there, thus buying time for the defeated wing to rally and support his immovable phalanx in the centre. However, Antiochus decided to flee once he heard and saw one wing of his army fleeing. As the Romans demonstrated (as had Ptolemy at Raphia), the flight of one wing of an army only leads to defeat if the rest of the army or the commander despairs and abandons the rest of the fight. The Romans rallied and fought back, whereas Antiochus simply turned and fled alongside his army. In doing so he abandoned the phalanx that was still ably holding firm in the centre.

Hindsight is a wonderful thing, but in view of the nature of the battlefield and the Roman line secured on the river, Antiochus should have stationed his best cavalry on his left and personally led a charge here to turn the Roman flank and eliminate their only significant cavalry force. The other flank even without his presence may well have broken the few Roman cavalry on that wing by sheer weight of numbers just as Antiochus did in the actual battle. Having thus gained cavalry superiority on both flanks, Antiochus could then have pressed on the Roman centre with his cavalry and light troops, leaving the phalanx relatively secure in a frontal assault on the Roman infantry.

Appian (*Syrian War* 32) actually criticized Antiochus for placing his hopes on his cavalry and not his phalanx, but this was the best way to defeat the Roman army and numerically Antiochus' overwhelming advantage. Had Antiochus gained cavalry success on both flanks, or at the very least nullified or routed Eumenes' expert cavalry force, he would perhaps have won the battle despite the prowess of the Roman infantry.

Antiochus should have learned from the prior successes of Hannibal, his advisor, and trusted to victory by surrounding the Roman infantry with cavalry. He had the cavalry forces to do so and had even better infantry to hold the centre than the Carthaginian army ever did. Yet his initial mistake of a chariot charge cost him any opportunity to even try. Perhaps the hardest lesson for a general to learn when it comes to combined arms is which unit to use when and how. Antiochus failed to learn that lesson despite the numerous historical examples before him and so lost the battle, the war and his hard-won western conquests.

Combined arms should have brought Antiochus victory. Instead, one single miscalculation concerning one single unit lost him everything.

Conclusion

The battles of Antiochus III the Great demonstrate perfectly how even the best-constructed armies still rely on the ability of their commanders to gain a victory. Antiochus' army was no different to those of the hundreds of Hellenistic generals that went before him. He inherited an experienced combined arms army with practised commanders. Yet in the major battles he fought he had only a 50-50 record of three wins and three losses (Apollonia, Arius and Panion versus Raphia, Thermopylae and Magnesia). Antiochus should never have fought at Thermopylae since he was so severely outnumbered and could never have won, but at both Raphia and Magnesia it was his own actions or initial tactics that snatched defeat from the jaws of victory.

On small things do great fortunes fall, but Antiochus was within reach of winning every equal confrontation that he fought. With a better grasp of controlling his own impulses to pursue the routed enemy after a cavalry charge (as at Raphia and Magnesia) and with a better understanding of the weaknesses of every unit (as at Magnesia) Antiochus could and perhaps should have won.

Though he earned his nickname for reaffirming Seleucid superiority over a large empire, when it comes to winning battles Antiochus was significantly inferior to his contemporaries as well as most Hellenistic generals before and after. He was arguably one of the finest ever at leading a cavalry charge to success, but he was at the same time one of the worst in history at turning a successful cavalry charge into an overall victory.

Taken as a whole, it is clear to see from this study that Antiochus was the reason for his eventual defeat to Rome. The Seleucid army and the Macedonian style of warfare reliant on a sarissa phalanx and heavy cavalry fighting together in a combined arms system was very capable of resisting Rome. Contrary to the contentions of modern Roman military historians and ancient historians of Rome such as Polybius, Livy and Appian, there was nothing inherently superior about the Roman way of war. Hellenistic commanders had demonstrated for more than a century that Macedonian-style combined arms worked well in combat on all types of terrain.

The difference was that Macedonian-style armies were complicated amalgamations of tens of different unit styles. Each individual unit had different strengths and weaknesses that needed to be harmonized together with the others if an army was to fight effectively. It took great tactical and strategic skill from generals and officers alike to properly utilize such a multifaceted army. Hellenistic history is littered with examples of such skilful commanders even among Antiochus' own contemporaries. Unfortunately, Antiochus was not one of them.

Philip V of Macedon proved to be a good general in winning many battles at a young age, despite his most famous defeat to the Romans at Cynoscephalae. Machanidas and Nabis, the tyrants of Sparta, led armies well before their final defeats to Philopoemen. Attalus I and Eumenes of Pergamum repeatedly demonstrated their abilities. Even Antiochus' enemy at Raphia, Ptolemy IV, showed how to win despite the loss of one wing.

Just before Antiochus became king, the Battle of Sellasia saw a gathering of great commanders on both sides. Cleomenes of Sparta led his army well, despite his defeat against Antigonus Doson, but the defeat was brought about by the initiative of the greatest general of the era, Philopoemen. More than anyone else in the late third and early second centuries he proved how important a reliable cavalry unit was in a Macedonian-style army. His career is a litany of successes and where he failed he quickly rescued the war with another victory. His last battle ended in defeat and capture and eventually his forced suicide. Yet even here he had won the initial confrontation and only fled when severely outnumbered on the arrival of enemy reinforcements. He gallantly held off pursuers on his own to save his men, but became separated in rough ground and, being thrown from his horse, he hit his head.

Philopoemen was the greatest general of his time, but almost all the other generals of note were better than Antiochus at focusing on overall victory rather than the personal glory of the charge. Perhaps Antiochus, like many others, was inspired by Alexander the Great's heroic exploits at the head of his cavalry, but Alexander always made sure that his generals and officers knew the battle plan before the battle so they could carry it out without him. Alexander always got the best out of every unit in his army, whatever the terrain or the occasion, and he always used a successful cavalry charge to expose the enemy's weak point and turn on the centre. All three of these great traits were precisely the skills that Antiochus lacked. Moreover, the lack of these skills is what led directly to his two great defeats at Raphia and Magnesia.

Antiochus' army demonstrated the effectiveness of combined arms in battle, but Antiochus himself proved that armies are only as successful as those leading them. This, in a final thought, brings us back to Iphicrates' description of a Greek army as body parts. He states that the head is the general. If you cut off the head, you defeat the army. However, if the head, or rather the brain within it, is not particularly astute then the whole body does not function properly and brings about its own downfall.

Antiochus desired to reconquer the empire of Alexander. If it were not for his blind love of the thrill of the pursuit, he had the opportunities to fulfil this ambition. Alas, such are the trials of men and kings. Fortune favours the bold but not the reckless. Antiochus twice charged too far and so his empire never stretched far enough.

Notes

Introduction

1. For recent analyses of Antiochus' empire see J. Grainger, *The Seleukid Empire of Antiochus III, 223–187 BC* (Barnsley, Pen & Sword, 2020) and M. Taylor, *Antiochus the Great* (Barnsley, Pen & Sword, 2013).
2. See below for an explanation of combined arms.
3. Diodorus, 16.85-86; Polyaenus, 4.2.2; Plutarch, *Alexander* 12 & *Demosthenes* 20. Philip's phalanx successfully pulled back up a slope in the face of the enemy. The cavalry on the left wing led by Alexander routed the Greek phalanx charging into gaps resulting from the Greek advance.
4. There is much debate as to the exact length of the sarissas in Macedonian armies. The earliest source, Theophrastus (*Hist. Pl.* 3.12.2), a contemporary of Philip II and Alexander the Great, lists the length of the longest sarissas as 12 cubits or just over 18ft. Asclepiodotus (*Tact.* 5.1), a Hellenistic writer of a tactical manual reflecting on Alexander the Great, lists the sarissa as short as 10 cubits or 15ft. Polybius (18.29-30) states that they were at longest 16 cubits (24ft) shortened to 14 cubits (21ft). Polyaenus (*Strat.* 2.29.2) states that the Spartan Cleomenes fielded a phalanx with 16-cubit sarissas. Thus, we can see that the sarissa lengthened under later generals. For a good analysis see J.R. Mixter, 'The Length of the Macedonian Sarissa during the Reigns of Philip II and Alexander the Great', *AncW* 23 (1992), 21-29.
5. See A.M. Snodgrass, *Early Greek Armour and Weapons from the End of the Bronze Age to 600 BC* (Edinburgh, Edinburgh University Press, 1964) for still the best description of Greek weapons and armour.
6. See A.M. Devine, 'The short sarissa again', *AncW* 27 (1996), 52-3 on the difference between short medieval pike heads and the larger heads excavated at Vergina.
7. Plutarch, *Aemilius Paullus* 16-22; Livy 44.40-42.
8. M. Andronikos, 'Sarissa', *BCH* 94 (1970), 91-107.
9. See W. Heckel, C. Willekes and G. Wrightson, 'Scythed Chariots at Gaugamela' in E. Carney and D. Ogden (eds), *Philip II and Alexander the Great: Father and Son, Lives and Afterlives* (Oxford, OUP, 2010), 103-113.
10. See below for a fuller discussion of Pydna.
11. It is not clear if Philip led a sarissa phalanx or javelin men at this battle against Onomarchus, the Phocian general of the Sacred War. There is only one source and it is not clear (Polyaenus, *Strat.* 2.38.2).

12. See E. Anson, 'Alexander's hypaspists and the *Argyraspids*', *Historia* 30 (1981), 117-20; E. Foulon, 'Hypaspistes, peltastes, chrysaspides, argyraspides, chalcaspides', *REA* 98 (1996), 53 63.

13. See C.A. Matthew, *An Invincible Beast: Understanding the Hellenistic Pike Phalanx in Action* (Barnsley, Pen & Sword, 2015).

14. See the photographs in this volume of the author's experiments with an 18ft sarissa.

15. See P. Connolly, 'Experiments with the sarissa – the Macedonian pike and cavalry lance – a functional view', *JRMES* 11 (2000), 103-12.

16. See G. Wrightson, 'To use or not to use: The practical and historical reliability of Asclepiodotus' "philosophical" tactical manual' in G. Lee, H. Whittaker & G. Wrightson (eds), *Ancient Warfare: Introducing Current Research* (*IAWC* vol. 1) (Cambridge Scholars Press, 2015), 65-93.

17. On integrated warfare, see G. Wrightson, 'Macedonian Armies and the Perfection of Combined Arms' in T. Howe, E. Garvin and G. Wrightson (eds), *Greece, Macedon and Persia: Studies in the Social, Political and Military Consequences of Conquest Societies in Honour of Waldemar Heckel* (Oxford, Oxbow, 2015), 59-68; and G. Wrightson, *Combined Arms Warfare in Ancient Greece from Homer to Alexander the Great and his Successors* (Oxford and New York, Routledge, 2019), 4-14.

18. See Wrightson, *Combined Arms*, 171-5.

19. For a detailed examination of elephants in late fourth-century combined arms armies, see Wrightson, 'Macedonian armies'.

20. On the nature of cataphracts, see D.T. Potts, '*Cataphractus* and *kamandar*: Some Thoughts on the Dynamic Evolution of Heavy Cavalry and Mounted Archers in Iran and Central Asia', *Bulletin of the Asia Institute* 21 (2007), 149-158.

21. On hamippoi in Alexander the Great's army see W. Heckel, 'The Royal Hypaspists in Battle: Macedonian *hamippoi*', *AHB* 26 (2012), 15-20.

22. In these versions the centre was actually weakened to tempt the enemy to attack it too enthusiastically and thus allow the encirclement to succeed. In the Macedonian style the centre was too strong to break but slow-moving enough to create time and space for the wings to encircle the enemy.

23. For more on this metaphor as it relates to combined arms see Wrightson, *Combined Arms*, 14-26.

24. This is similar to early modern army regiments known by the name of their commanding officer. For an analysis of the officer's position in commanding from the rear, a novelty in ancient warfare, see G. Wrightson, 'The nature of command in the Macedonian sarissa phalanx', *AHB* 24 (2010), 71-92.

25. See also A.M. Devine, 'The Pawn-Sacrifice at the Battle of the Granicus: The Origins of a Favourite Stratagem of Alexander the Great', *AncW* 18 (1988), 3-20.

26. For the best analyses of Alexander's manoeuvres at Gaugamela (Arrian, *Anabasis* 3.8-15; Curtius 4.9; Diodorus 17.56-61), see most recently Wrightson, *Combined Arms*, 193-7.
27. Paraitacene: Diodorus 19.26-31. Gabiene: Diodorus 19.39-43; Plutarch, *Eumenes* 16. For these two battles see A.M. Devine, 'Diodorus' Account of the Battle of Paraitacene (317 B.C.)', *Ancient World* 12 (1985), 75-86 and A.M. Devine, 'Diodorus' Account of the Battle of Gabiene', *Ancient World* 12 (1985), 87-96 and Wrightson, *Combined Arms*, 204-210.
28. This is not clear as the sources state the enemy came off the walls to chase the soldiers of Perdiccas who had foolishly allowed his men to get out of control, but this seems like later negative propaganda towards Perdiccas, who was one of Alexander's most trusted and capable officers. See B. Antela-Bernárdez, 'Furious Wrath: Alexander's Siege of Thebes and Perdiccas' False Retreat' in G. Lee, H. Whittaker & G. Wrightson (eds), *Ancient Warfare: Introducing Current Research* (*IAWC* vol. 1) (Cambridge Scholars Press, 2015), 94-106.
29. The famous historian W.W. Tarn was the first to argue this as Seleucus' intention: Tarn, 'Two Notes on Seleucid History: 1. Seleucus' 500 Elephants', *JHS* 60 (1940), 87 n. 1; Tarn, *Hellenistic Military and Naval Developments* (Chicago, Ares, 1975) 68-9. Bar Kochba gives a more nuanced analysis including the terrain and Demetrius' intentions: B. Bar Kochba, *The Seleucid Army* (Cambridge, CUP, 1976), 109-110.
30. Bar Kochba argues that the feigned withdrawal and surprise ambuscades were common tactics of the Seleucids, but the sources for the battles he lists as proof of this do not state that such surprises occurred. These are Cyrrhestica (286 under Seleucus I), against the Galatians (275 under Antiochus I), against Molon (220 under Antiochus III), and Elasa (160 under Demetrius I). These are all major battles not very well depicted in the sources. There are certainly other minor examples that Bar Kochba ignores just as Antiochus at Atabyrium, but I have yet to document them all fully.

Chapter One

1. See W. Heckel, 'Demetrios Poliorketes and the Diadochoi', *La parola del passato* 39 (1984), 438-440.
2. BM 34428 = Sp. II (I.L. Finkel, R.J. van der Spek and R. Pirngruber, *Babylonian Chronographic Texts from the Hellenistic Period* (2020) 11.
3. BM 32235 and BM 32957 (*BCHP* 9).
4. *Sudas. v. Simonides of Magnesia*, ed. Adler IV, 362 lines 21-23 = *FGrH* 163F = *Suppl. Hell.* 723.
5. See, for example, the coin of Antiochus III in this volume featuring an elephant.
6. Bar Kochba 76 suggests that the elephants died in travelling through Cappadocia.

7. All translations of Polybius are from the translation by Thayer for the Loeb edition.
8. Paraitacene: Diodorus 19.26 31. Gabiene: Diodorus 19.39-43; Plutarch, *Eumenes* 16.

Chapter Two

1. For the internecine rivalries in Antiochus' court see R. Strootman, 'Hellenistic Court Society: The Seleukid Imperial Court under Antiochos the Great, 223–187 BCE' in J. Duindam, T. Artan and M. Kunt (eds), *Royal Courts in Dynastic States and Empires: A Global Perspective. Rulers & Elites*, Volume 1, 63-89 (Leiden, Brill, 2011).
2. On this decade of eastern problems for the Seleucids and especially concerning the rise of Parthia, see in particular N. Overtoom, 'The Power-Transition Crisis of the 240s BCE and the Creation of the Parthian State', *The International History Review* 38, no. 5 (2016), 984-1013.
3. On Bactria and the other Eastern Greek kingdoms see R. Mairs (ed.), *The Graeco-Bactrian and Indo-Greek World* (New York and Oxford, Routledge, 2020).
4. This and all the following quotations from Polybius come from Book 5, section 65.
5. Peltasts as elite heavy infantry see F.W. Walbank, *Philip V of Macedon* (Cambridge, CUP, 1940), 290-293. First from G. Griffith, *The Mercenaries of the Hellenistic World* (New York, CUP, 1935), 319. See also G. Griffith, 'Peltast and the origins of the Macedonian phalanx' in H. Dell (ed.), *Ancient Macedonian studies in honour of Charles F. Edson* (Thessaloniki, Institute for Balkan Studies, 1953), 161-7. Walbank (*A historical commentary on Polybius*, Vol. 1 (Oxford and New York, OUP, 1970), 518 (- cf. 274 on Polyb. 2.65.2) in commentary on Philip V's use of peltasts (Polybius 4.64.3-11) states that the peltasts were armed as hypaspists with shield and spear just as under Alexander cf. W. Heckel, 'Synaspismos, Sarissas and Wagons', *Acta Classica* 48 (2005), 189-94. For peltasts as hypaspists see in particular Foulon; L. Ueda-Sarson, 'The evolution of the Hellenistic infantry, part 2: infantry of the successors', *Slingshot* 223 (2002), 23-8.
6. These subsequent quotations all follow in order, Polybius *Histories* 5.79.
7. Parmenion received significant criticism from the ancient historians about his conduct and request for aid at Gaugamela. Plutarch (*Alexander* 32) even called his actions sluggish and ineffectual: 'Many have blamed Parmenion for being sluggish and ineffectual in this battle, either because old age had already undermined his bravery or, as Callisthenes says, he was depressed and envious of the authority and self-importance of Alexander's power. At this point, the king, although he was annoyed by the summons, did not tell his soldiers the truth, but recalled his forces on the grounds that it was

dark and he wanted to stop the slaughtering. As he rode towards the part of his forces that was in danger, he heard as he was travelling that the enemy had been completely vanquished and was in flight.' This is certainly anti-Parmenion propaganda by Callisthenes after his execution.

8. For a good recent biography of Rupert, see Charles Spencer, *Prince Rupert: The Last Cavalier* (London, Weidenfeld & Nicolson, 2007), though some of the earlier biographies deal more with his military abilities.

Chapter Three

1. Polybius refers to the pact repeatedly. Livy references it in his description of the build-up to the Second Macedonian War, Livy 31.14.
2. For a detailed discussion of the pact and relevant literature, see A. Eckstein, 'The Pact Between the Kings, Polybius 15.20.6, and Polybius' View of the Outbreak of the Second Macedonian War' *Classical Philology* 100, No. 3 (July 2005), 228-242.
3. As above see Heckel et al. for an analysis of how horses and animals react to sarissas.

Chapter Four

1. Antiochus had begun to distrust Hannibal after he learned that Hannibal had had private conversations with Roman commissioners previously at Ephesus (Livy 35.14).
2. The Achaeans, according to Livy (35.30), viewed Philopoemen as equal to or even superior to Scipio Africanus because of his defeat of Nabis. I will analyze briefly Philopoemen's generalship in the following chapter in a summary of combined arms in Greece before Antiochus' arrival.
3. Scholars are often very concerned with the propagandistic nature of this marriage for establishing Seleucid dominance over newly-conquered territory for the first time. It also established Antiochus' new dominion in Greece. Scholars also rightly criticize the pro-Roman sources' views that Antiochus wasted a winter in debauched celebrations of a pointless marriage rather than preparing for war. See for a recent example and older bibliography on the topic M.S. Visscher, 'Poets and Politics: Antiochos the Great, Hegesianax and the War with Rome' in A. Coskun and D. Engels (eds), *Rome and the Seleukid East: Selected Papers from Seleukid Study Day V Brussels, 21-23 August 2015*, 61-85 (Brussels, Latomus, 2019). Clearly renaming his bride Euboia represents that. I do not seek to counter these arguments but rather to emphasize that Antiochus did neglect his military duties in favour of propaganda and that, indeed, was extremely detrimental to his ongoing war effort against Rome, just as the pro-Roman historians discuss.
4. E. Gruen, *The Hellenistic World and the Coming of Rome* (Berkeley, LA, London, California University Press, 1984).

5. Gruen, 461. Aetolians at Thermopylae: Livy, 36.15.2-5; Appian, *Syr.* 18.
6. The fullest examination of Antiochus' and Rome's stance in the preliminaries to the war is J. Grainger, *The Roman War of Antiochus the Great* (Leiden and Boston, Brill, 2002), but Grainger goes too far to mitigate Antiochus' blunders as the result of anti-Seleucid propaganda in the pro-Roman sources. Though I admit the sources are biased against Antiochus, his bewildering and chaotic strategy, if there is even an overriding one, still exists despite the bias. See also Gruen, 620-636.
7. N. Rosenstein, *Rome and the Mediterranean, 290 to 146 BC* (Edinburgh, Edinburgh University Press, 2012) 195.

Chapter Five

1. Arrian, *Anabasis* 1.12-16; Diodorus 17.19-21; Plutarch, *Alexander* 16; Justin 11.6.
2. Arrian, *Anabasis* 2.7-11; Curtius 3.8-11; Diodorus 17.32-4; Plutarch, *Alexander* 20; Justin 11.9.
3. Plutarch, *Pyrrhus* 16-7; Zonaras 8.3; Orosius 4.1; Livy, *Epitome* 13.
4. Livy 32.5-6 and 10-12; Plutarch, *Flamininus* 3-5.
5. Polybius 11.11-8; Pausanias 8.50.
6. N.G.L. Hammond, 'The two battles of Chaeronea: 338 BC and 86 BC', *Klio* 31 (1938), 186-218. Cynoscephalae: Polybius 18.19-26; Livy 33.6-10; Plutarch, *Flamininus* 7-8.
7. Polybius 2.65-9; Plutarch, *Cleomenes* 27-8; Plutarch, *Philopoemen* 6.
8. Plutarch, *Pyrrhus* 24-5; Orosius 4.2; Livy, *Epitome* 14; Dionysius of Halicarnassus, *Roman Antiquities* 20.10-11.
9. Plutarch, *Aemilius Paullus* 16-22; Livy 44.40-2.
10. Xenophon, *Anabasis* 4.8.9-19; Asclepiodotus, *Tact.* 11.7. On Xenophon, see Wrightson, *Combined Arms*, 143-4; on Asclepiodotus, see Wrightson, 'To use or not to use', 87.
11. Much has been written about the Roman republican army and the maniple, but in particular on the maniple see M. Taylor, 'Roman Infantry Tactics in the Mid-Republic: A Reassessment', *Historia* 63 (2014), 301-322; and most recently M. Taylor, 'The Evolution of the Manipular Legion in the Early Republic', *Historia* 69 (2020/1), 38-56.
12. Wrightson, 'Macedonian armies'.
13. For analysis see Wrightson, 'The Nature of Command'.
14. See the images in this book.
15. Heckel, 'The Royal Hypaspists' and G. Wrightson, '"Surprise, surprise": The tactical response of Alexander to guerrilla warfare and fighting in difficult terrain', *The Ancient World* 46, no. 2 (2015), 162-179.

Chapter Seven

1. On Raphia see above as well as J. Pietrykowski, *Great Battles of the Hellenistic World* (Barnsley, Pen & Sword, 2009), 181-194.

2. Anyone wanting to more fully understand the Roman legion fighting system should play the computer game 'Rome: Total War'. It perfectly exemplifies the Roman army units, deployment and fighting styles. It also allows someone to discover the best ways to defeat such a strong infantry force. A hint: it involves combined arms! The game also allows you to command armies in historical battles that are mostly true to the descriptions in the primary sources.

Chapter Eight

1. For a comparison note the success of the Crusaders in the defence of Antioch during the First Crusade where a force of 1,000 knights charged out of the city and routed the Muslim army of tens of thousands. So surprising was the victory to the Crusaders that they believed a saint rode before them on an angelic stallion, which caused all before them to flee.

2. In fact, it was Eumenes who really instigated the Roman war on Antiochus and who benefited at its conclusion with an enormous increase in power, land and prestige to become the most powerful monarch in Asia Minor. See e.g. Gruen, 542-550, esp. 546: 'This was more Eumenes' war than the Senate's. He stood to gain most from it – and he made his wishes felt.' It is therefore perhaps fitting that Eumenes justified his position as prime motivator and beneficiary by being the principal reason for the decisive Roman victory at Mantinea. He tried the same tactic against the increasing threat of Perseus by prompting Rome to declare the Third Macedonian War, again to benefit Pergamum, cf. Gruen, 556.

Bibliography

Andronikos, M., 'Sarissa', *BCH* 94 (1970), 91-107.

Anson, E., 'Alexander's hypaspists and the Argyraspids', *Historia* 30 (1981), 117-20.

Antela-Bernárdez, B., 'Furious Wrath: Alexander's Siege of Thebes and Perdiccas' False Retreat' in G. Lee, H. Whittaker & G. Wrightson (eds), *Ancient Warfare: Introducing Current Research* (*IAWC*, vol. 1), 94-106 (Cambridge Scholars Press, 2015)

Bar Kochba, B., *The Seleucid Army* (Cambridge, CUP, 1976)

Connolly, P., 'Experiments with the sarissa – the Macedonian pike and cavalry lance – a functional view', *JRMES* 11 (2000), 103-12.

Devine, A.M., 'Diodorus' Account of the Battle of Paraitacene (317 B.C.)', *Ancient World* 12 (1985), 75-86.

—— 'Diodorus' Account of the Battle of Gabiene', *Ancient World* 12 (1985), 87-96.

—— 'The Pawn-Sacrifice at the Battle of the Granicus: The Origins of a Favourite Stratagem of Alexander the Great', *AncW* 18 (1988), 3-20.

Eckstein, A., 'The Pact Between the Kings, Polybius 15.20.6, and Polybius' View of the Outbreak of the Second Macedonian War', *Classical Philology* 100, No. 3 (July 2005), 228-242.

Finkel, I.L., Van der Spek, R.J. and Pirngruber, R., *Babylonian Chronographic Texts from the Hellenistic Period* (2020)

Foulon, E., 'Hypaspistes, peltastes, chrysaspides, argyraspides, chalcaspides', *REA* 98 (1996), 53-63.

Grainger, J., *The Roman War of Antiochus the Great* (Leiden & Boston, Brill, 2002)

—— *The Seleukid Empire of Antiochus III, 223–187 BC* (Barnsley, Pen & Sword, 2020)

Griffith, G., *The Mercenaries of the Hellenistic World* (New York, CUP, 1935)

—— 'Peltast and the origins of the Macedonian phalanx' in H. Dell (ed.), *Ancient Macedonian studies in honour of Charles F. Edson*, 161-7 (Thessaloniki, Institute for Balkan Studies, 1953)

Gruen, E., *The Hellenistic World and the Coming of Rome* (Berkeley, LA, London, California University Press, 1984)

Hammond, N.G.L., 'The two battles of Chaeronea: 338 BC and 86 BC', *Klio* 31 (1938), 186-218.

Heckel, W., 'Demetrios Poliorketes and the Diadochoi', *La parola del passato* 39 (1984), 438-440.

—— 'Synaspismos, Sarissas and Wagons', *Acta Classica* 48 (2005), 189-94.

—— 'The Royal Hypaspists in Battle: Macedonian *hamippoi*', *AHB* 26 (2012), 15-20.

Heckel, W., Willekes, C. & Wrightson, G., 'Scythed Chariots at Gaugamela' in E. Carney and D. Ogden (eds), *Philip II and Alexander the Great: Father and Son, Lives and Afterlives*, 103-113 (Oxford, OUP, 2010)

Mairs, R., (ed.), *The Graeco-Bactrian and Indo-Greek World* (New York & Oxford, Routledge, 2020)

Matthew, C.A., *An Invincible Beast: Understanding the Hellenistic Pike Phalanx in Action* (Barnsley, Pen & Sword, 2015)

Mixter, J.R., 'The Length of the Macedonian Sarissa during the Reigns of Philip II and Alexander the Great', *AncW* 23 (1992), 21-29.

Overtoom, N., 'The Power-Transition Crisis of the 240s BCE and the Creation of the Parthian State', *The International History Review* 38, no. 5 (2016), 984-1013.

Pietrykowski, J., *Great Battles of the Hellenistic World* (Barnsley, Pen & Sword, 2009)

Potts, D.T., '*Cataphractus* and *kamandar*: Some thoughts on the dynamic evolution of Heavy Cavalry and Mounted Archers in Iran and Central Asia', *Bulletin of the Asia Institute* 21 (2007), 149-158.

Rosenstein, N., *Rome and the Mediterranean 290 to 146 BC* (Edinburgh, Edinburgh University Press, 2012)

Snodgrass, A.M., *Early Greek Armour and Weapons from the End of the Bronze Age to 600 BC* (Edinburgh, Edinburgh University Press, 1964)

Spencer, C., *Prince Rupert: The Last Cavalier* (London, Weidenfeld & Nicolson, 2007)

Strootman, R., 'Hellenistic Court Society: The Seleukid Imperial Court Under Antiochos The Great, 223–187 BCE' in J. Duindam, T. Artan and M. Kunt (eds), *Royal Courts in Dynastic States and Empires: A Global Perspective. Rulers & Elites*, Volume 1, 63-89 (Leiden, Brill, 2011)

Tarn, W.W., 'Two Notes on Seleucid History: 1. Seleucus' 500 Elephants', *JHS* 60 (1940), 24-94.

—— *Hellenistic Military and Naval Developments* (Chicago, Ares, 1975)

Taylor, M., *Antiochus the Great* (Barnsley, Pen & Sword, 2013)

—— 'Roman Infantry Tactics in the Mid-Republic: A Reassessment', *Historia* 63 (2014), 301-322.

—— 'The Evolution of the Manipular Legion in the Early Republic', *Historia* 69 (2020/1), 38-56.

Ueda-Sarson, L., 'The evolution of the Hellenistic infantry part 2: infantry of the Successors', *Slingshot* 223 (2002), 23-8.

Visscher, M.S., 'Poets and Politics: Antiochos the Great, Hegesianax and the War with Rome' in A. Coskun and D. Engels (eds), *Rome and the Seleukid East: Selected Papers from Seleukid Study Day V, Brussels, 21-23 August 2015*, 61-85 (Brussels, Latomus, 2019).

Walbank, F.W., *Philip V of Macedon* (Cambridge, CUP, 1940)

— *A historical commentary on Polybius*, Vol. 1 (Oxford & New York, OUP, 1970)

Wrightson, G., 'The nature of command in the Macedonian sarissa phalanx', *AHB* 24 (2010), 71-92.

— 'To use or not to use: The practical and historical reliability of Asclepiodotus' "philosophical" tactical manual' in G. Lee, H. Whittaker & G. Wrightson (eds), *Ancient Warfare: Introducing Current Research* (*IAWC*, vol. 1), 65-93 (Cambridge Scholars Press, 2015).

— 'Macedonian armies and the perfection of Combined Arms' in T. Howe, E. Garvin & G. Wrightson (eds), *Greece, Macedon and Persia: Studies in the Social, Political and Military Consequences of Conquest Societies in honour of Waldemar Heckel*, 59-68 (Oxford, Oxbow, 2015).

— '"Surprise, surprise": The tactical response of Alexander to guerrilla warfare and fighting in difficult terrain', *Ancient World* 46, no. 2 (2015), 162-179.

— *Combined Arms Warfare in Ancient Greece from Homer to Alexander the Great and his Successors* (Oxford & New York, Routledge, 2019)

Index

Index of Names

Index of Places

Index of Battles and Sieges